# Prayer

## BEARING THE WORLD AS JESUS DID

# Prayer

## BEARING THE WORLD
## AS JESUS DID

DENNIS F. KINLAW
AND CHRISTIANE ALBERTSON

Francis Asbury Press
Distributed by Warner Press
Anderson, Indiana

Coordinator of Publishing & Creative Services
Church of God Ministries, Inc.
PO Box 2420
Anderson, IN 46018-2420
800-848-2464 • www.chog.org

To purchase additional copies of this book, to inquire about distribution, and for all other sales-related matters, please contact:

Warner Press, Inc.
PO Box 2499
Anderson, IN 46018-2499
800-741-7721 • www.warnerpress.org

ISBN-13: 978-1-59317-614-3

Printed in the United States of America.

13 14 15 16 17 / CH / 10 9 8 7 6 5 4 3 2

# TABLE OF CONTENTS

# I

# THE HEART OF
# INTERCESSORY PRAYER

## GOD GIVES US THE PRIVILEGE
## OF BEING PARTNERS IN HIS WORK.

While on a trip to Florida several years ago, I was invited to appear on a Christian television program. The studio was in St. Petersburg, and I was supposed to arrive forty-five minutes early so I could be briefed on what I was supposed to do. Unfortunately, we were detained in traffic, so we walked into the studio thirty seconds after the program had begun. I had no idea what the interviewer was going to ask me. After a few minutes of introductory conversation, he asked, "What is the most staggering thought you have ever found in your walk with God and your study of Scripture?"

I sat for a moment, uncertain how to respond. Then I said, "The most staggering thing I have ever learned is that the eternal God—who is Father, Son, and Holy Spirit—has invited me to enter into conversation with that exclusive group."

The interviewer stared at me for a long moment and then said, "That does sort of blow you away, doesn't it?"

His answer was exactly right, of course. God's invitation for us to be part of his triune conversation certainly ought to blow our minds. The marvelous reality is that a person like me can come to know God personally, in a communion so intimate that I take part in God's inner conversational life. Most of us do not anticipate that depth of relationship when we first come to know him. He wants us as part of his life, and that is what salvation is, but he also calls us and gives us the privilege of being partners in his work. God's call, as Paul says, is that we should become "workers together with him" (2 Cor 6:1 KJV). This calling is what theologians term *election*. It intimates what human history is all about, the very ultimate purpose of human existence. And it all begins with the Old Testament story of a man the biblical narrators said "walked with God." I refer to the story of Abraham.

## ABRAHAM: FRIEND OF GOD

Abraham is seventy-five years old when we get the first record of God conversing with him. Abraham was quite successful in life, except in one respect: he and his wife, Sarah, had no children. That meant they had no future progeny, a tragedy then just as it is now.

In Abraham's day, the true God was unknown. Human beings worshiped the forces of nature with which they struggled daily and called them "gods." One day the true God came to Abraham and told him he was going to look on him with favor. God promised that Abraham and his wife Sarah were going to have a son who would father a great nation. This would be a special nation through which all others would be blessed or cursed. God told Abraham that his name would become great and that ultimately, through his descendants, God would send One through whom blessing would come to all the peoples on the earth. With that encounter, a friendship began to develop between Abraham and God that deepened across the years. Their relationship was such that Abraham was the first person in the Bible to be called a "friend" of God (2 Chron 20:7; Isa 41:8; James 2:23).

Periodically, God reminded Abraham of this promise. Twenty-four years after their first recorded conversation, God comes to him again. Abraham is now ninety-nine years old and his wife is eighty-nine. God tells him that Sarah will conceive in this year and the next year she will bear the long-awaited son. This is a time of great joy for Abraham and Sarah, but apparently it was also a time of great joy for God himself. We can make this inference because, in a previous conversation, God told Abraham his son must be named Isaac.

The Hebrew name transliterated by our English word *Isaac* is a verb that literally means "He laughs." Normally, an ancient Near Eastern name was actually a sentence. We see this in biblical names like Michael, Nathaniel, or Gabriel. Michael is perfect Hebrew. *Mi* is the Hebrew pronoun "who," *cha* in Hebrew means "like," and *el* is the word for "God." So Mi-cha-el means "Who is like God?" It is really a praise name. Nathaniel means "God has given," and Gabriel, "Man of God." In each of these names, the subject of the sentence is God. This was typical of a Hebrew name in Abraham's day. It is therefore fair to assume that the name Isaac ("He laughs") meant that God himself laughed for joy. And why would God laugh? Because Isaac was the beginning of the messianic line that would ultimately produce Jesus of Nazareth, through whom God would win his lost world back to himself.

So this story is of no small significance in terms of God's eternal purposes and of human history. The God who visits Abraham and develops a friendship with him is the God who wants to redeem his world and he will do it through a descendant of Abraham—Jesus. In this story, God is clearly the-God-Who-Saves. But there is more to the story.

## ABRAHAM'S INVITATION TO PRAY

This conversation between God and his friend occurs at a meal in Abraham's tent. When the conversation is over and God is ready to go on his way, Abraham in good courtesy walks with him to the edge of the camp. We get a remarkable account of what happens as they walk. It occupies only four verses, but it casts its shadow across the rest of human history. God is talking to himself, and he allows Abraham to eavesdrop on his conversation.

The conversation reveals that God, who is the friend of Abraham, is not only the Creator of the world whose purposes are always to redeem; he is also the-Judge-of-All-the-Earth, the ultimate guarantor of justice in the world (Gen 18:25). God has heard that the cities of Sodom and Gomorrah are places where evil in the forms of injustice, rapine, and murder reign. His concern for the welfare of the innocent and his anger at the wanton immorality of these cities are so great that he, the guarantor of ultimate righteousness, must investigate. This may mean the destruction of two great cities. So God talks to himself.

He asks, "Shall I hide from Abraham what I am about to do?" (Gen 18:17). He concludes that he must not. His reason? The descendants of Abraham are the key to the ultimate blessing of the world. They will be his means through which he will reveal himself to a world that does not know him and win it back to himself. That ultimate redemption of humanity will come through Abraham's family, which will become a "kingdom of priests and a holy nation" (Ex 19:6) who are called to bring the whole world to a knowledge of the one true God. God says to himself that he must share his burden with his friend because Abraham, too, is involved. So God discloses his intentions to Abraham, and God's burden becomes Abraham's burden.

Then we read the account of Abraham's intercession for Sodom and Gomorrah. He begins by insisting that it is not God's nature to destroy righteous people along with the unrighteous, so Abraham reasons that if there are even as few as fifty righteous people in the two cities, God should save the cities. God agrees. Notice the principle: Righteous people may be the means of salvation for those who are not righteous. A biblical principle is being laid down here: one's welfare ultimately depends on another.

Abraham keeps reasoning with God until he gets down to ten, and God agrees that if there are ten righteous people, he will not destroy the cities. At ten Abraham stops. We do not know what would have happened if Abraham had continued his intercession. However, for the moment, the survival of two great cities hangs on one human being and his intercession. Uncharacteristically, Abraham is concerned more about others than he is about himself.

Examine the previous interactions between Abraham and God and you will notice that the initiative had always been with God and the conversations were always about what Abraham would receive from this friendship. But here on the edge of Abraham's camp, Abraham does something extraordinary. He prays earnestly *for others*. True, his prime thought may have been for his nephew Lot and his family; but even if saving his own family was Abraham's motive, he was pleading for someone other than himself.

The potential for good is staggering when anyone gets out of his or her own self. We are being introduced to a principle that will permeate the rest of Scripture. It is what I call *the mediatorial principle.* This is the principle that says everyone's salvation rests on another and, therefore, depends on the intercession of another. When we get to the crux point in human history, we will find that the salvation of us all rests on one other person, whose name is Jesus. The redemption of the world then moves from what Jesus did for us all to what he can do when his saving power is allowed to flow out to other people through those who live in him.

Jesus makes it clear in his high priestly prayer (John 17) that the world will come to know who he is through those who come to believe because of the disciples. And the prime condition for it all is found in prayer. Yes, prayer is really that crucial for the world.

Another angle of this story has been significant for me. It was my privilege for several years to teach Hebrew, so I often found myself reading this text in Hebrew. I noticed that when God had finished telling Abraham about the possible destruction of the two cities, the Hebrew text says "Abraham remained standing before the Lord." (Gen 18:22 NRSV). This implies that Abraham realizes the seriousness of the moment and what it could mean to his nephew and his family, as well as to the two great cities. So he ponders the situation and then begins interceding with the Lord.

However, the Hebrew text of that verse has a footnote. When I checked the footnote, I found that the scribal tradition suggested a different original reading. Seldom did copyists ever feel free to amend the text of Scripture. They believed the text was too holy for that. Yet there are at least eighteen places in the Old Testament where they did actually amend the text, and one of them is found in this verse. The footnote stated that the original text of this verse says it was God who "remained standing before Abraham" when they reached the edge of the camp. If that reading is true, it gives us a very different picture of what happened. If Abraham "remained standing before the LORD," we get the impression that Abraham is thinking, *Is there anything I can say that would make a difference?* But if God "remained standing before Abraham," God might have been thinking, *Isn't Abraham going to say anything else? He has a nephew and a family down there, and he has just heard that they will be destroyed.* In that case, the intercession was initiated by God and not by Abraham.

That would be consistent with the biblical teaching that from the beginning, the initiative for our salvation started not with us but with God. In our fallen state, we have no proper concern for others. It must be quickened in us by the Holy Spirit. The kind of love that can make a difference in someone else's life never originates with us. It must be, as Paul says, God's own love "poured out . . . into our hearts" (Rom 5:5). Nothing *saving* ever originates with us. It always starts with God, because he alone is the Savior. The love of God, which binds the three persons of the Trinity together and cares for our lost world, is placed in our hearts by God's Spirit. It is different enough from the best of human love that the biblical writers developed a special word, agape, to denote it. The common words for love everyone in the Greek-speaking world used, even for the noblest of human affections, simply were not adequate.

Perhaps an ancient Hebrew writer who had never read the story of the cross or the second chapter of Philippians would feel there was something incongruous about the King-of-All-the-Earth standing before a human being, imploring him by his posture to intercede for his own kind. An ancient Near Eastern king normally received requests sitting on his throne while the petitioner stood before him. But the God who comes to visit Abraham, shares his burden with him, and now stands waiting for him to speak, is the-God-Who-Saves. He is the kind of father who does not wait for the prodigal to come home but goes into the far country to get him. What we see in this story is not found in any other religion of the world. Our God so longs for us to be members of his own family that he makes us in his own likeness, allows us to know him personally, and counts us significant enough that he invites us to join him in his great work of redemption. The first picture of our role in God's kingdom is not one of prophecy or preaching; those will come later. The initial picture is that of intercession. Why do we so often miss this point?

If the welfare of two great cities rested in the hands of Abraham, whose welfare rests in yours and mine? And are our hands praying hands?

## God's Initiative Toward Us

Perhaps a further word is appropriate here. We have said that God takes the initiative in everything that is saving. We are the ones who need to be saved, but the initiative to do something about our need never originates with us. The initiative comes from God, who has the answer to our need. Our role is always response. We should never forget this. There is no indication that Abraham was seeking God when the Lord went to him the first time. We are simply told that God went to Abraham and told him to leave his country and follow him. Moses was not seeking God when the bush burned and caught his attention. He was deep in Midian, fleeing from the wrath of Pharaoh, when God caught his attention and got him to listen. This is the biblical pattern. God is the shepherd who goes into the wilderness to find one lost sheep. God is the eternal Son who comes to earth to reach people who have lost their way. He is the King who knocks at the door of our hearts when we should be the ones knocking at his door, seeking admission. He is the God who goes to visit Abraham. He is the-God-Who-Saves and the-God-Who-Seeks.

The truth of this came home rather dramatically to me one day on an airplane flight.

When I was in the administration of Asbury College, our board chairman lived in San Antonio, Texas. From time to time, it was my responsibility to go to Texas and talk college business with him. My usual pattern was to fly from Kentucky to Atlanta, where I could catch a nonstop flight to San Antonio. One day when I got to Atlanta, I found the flight to San Antonio was already booked full. I had to take another flight to Houston, where I could get a flight on to San Antonio.

As I boarded the plane in Houston, I noticed two empty seats in a row where a young man already had the window seat. I took the aisle seat. I noticed that on the seat between us was a stack of maps of Mexico City. I also noticed that the young man next to the window was lost in a paperback history of Mexico. He was not only reading; he was also annotating the book. He had a red pencil and would occasionally mark as he read. He was an attractive young person, and I wondered about his interest in Mexico. I thought he might be a missionary, so I asked, "Is that a good history of Mexico?"

He responded, "It is the best one I have found," and handed it to me.

I noticed as I examined the book that his handwriting was clear, his spelling was good, and his sentence structure flawless. I thought, *This guy is well-educated.* He was marking the book as if he were a university student preparing for a big exam. So I asked, "Why are you interested in Mexico?"

His response caught me off guard. "I am a high school janitor in Chicago and I have a month's vacation. I decided to spend it seeing Mexico City and its environs by foot and public transportation." As you can easily imagine, I was all the more intrigued with my man.

He then asked, "And what are you reading?" I had in my hands a dusty old copy of Augustine's work on the Trinity. As I handed it to him, I thought, *This will surely turn off a high school janitor from Chicago!* But I misjudged him again. He looked at it and then turned rather quickly and asked, "Are you a Christian?"

I responded affirmatively and returned the question, quite confident that he would say he was. To my surprise, his response was, "No. I am an atheist—or at least I think I am." Surprised, I said nothing for a moment, but he was not ready to let the conversation stop. His next question was, "Since you are a Christian, do you believe in prayer?"

"Yes," I responded. "At my house we believe in prayer."

Immediately, he asked, "Why?"

We had just gone through a very unusual experience in our family. Our son was doing a residency in surgery. One day while he was operating with two other doctors, replacing the heart valve in a patient who, incidentally, had a florid case of hepatitis, he was accidentally struck with a suture needle, inoculating him with the hepatitis virus.

In due time, our son came down with the hepatitis from which the girl had been suffering. When the medical school officials found out Denny was infected, they scrubbed him out of surgery and sent him home. So we put him, his wife, and their baby in our guest room to care for him. We watched his health deteriorate. In spite of his doctors' best efforts, multiple liver biopsies just confirmed that he was only getting worse, and the doctors had nothing further to offer. Some friends came in, anointed him with oil, and prayed for him. Then God healed him. I told my new friend that story and said again, "Yes, we believe in prayer at our house."

Both of us sat silent for a few moments. Then he surprised me again. He said quite simply, "I think I believe in prayer too." Needless to say, I asked why, and he told me his story.

He had had a problem with severe headaches. He sought medical help, but the headaches actually worsened. They became so intense that he did not think he could bear them. He even considered suicide. He reflected that religious people who have great problems pray and some of them say it helps. So he thought, *Before I commit suicide, perhaps I, too, should pray.*

But how does an atheist pray? He decided to try. He said to the God he did not think existed, "I do not know whether or not you are; and if you are, I do not know whether or not you could help me; and if you could help me, I do not know whether or not you would. But if you are, and if you could, and if you would, there would be one guy very grateful."

The headaches went away. His response to that was, "What a lucky coincidence!"

However, he became quite unhappy with his response. He thought, *What if there is someone out there who did that for me and I attribute it to chance? That is a cheap way out.* So he prayed again. He said to God, "I do not know whether or not you are, and I do not know whether or not you healed me. But if you are and if you did, I want you to know my gratitude."

"Funny," he said, "I suddenly began to think of other serendipities in my life that came to me unexpectedly and undeserved, and I thought, *What if there is somebody out there and he has been doing these things for me all along and I have never even thanked him?* So he prayed again to the God he was not sure existed—and thanked him for unrecognized blessings! By now I was entranced. He turned and asked, "Do you think our conversation is an accident?"

I laughed and said, "Oh, no! I am not even supposed to be on this plane."

"That's funny. I am not either. When I bought my ticket in Chicago, they said it was for a nonstop flight from Chicago to Mexico City. Then I found that we had to make a stop in Houston and San Antonio before going on to Mexico City." He concluded, "I am not supposed to be on this flight either, so I don't think this conversation is an accident."

Right about that moment, I felt the plane shudder and realized that we had landed. I was so moved by the conversation that I had lost all track of time. I realized that in just a moment we would be at the gate, so I found myself saying to God, "You can't let this conversation stop now. I just have him to the place where I can really tell him about you."

Then I seemed to hear the inner Voice saying, "Well, Kinlaw, I was doing pretty well with him before you came along." And, of course, he was.

Since that day, I have realized that I am never the first witness in anyone's life. God is always at work in another person before I get there. God's witness to himself is the first, and he is actively there after I leave.

Old Testament law said a person could not be convicted of a crime unless there were two witnesses. So I have come to think of my witness as the second one, which merely confirms what God already is saying in another person's life. The initiative is with God, because he is love itself. Redemptive love is his very nature. That does not mean that our second witness does not count. It does. And it is important. How important? That is what we will look at next.

# 2

## PERSONHOOD AND THE DIVINE PRESENCE

IF WE WORK ON OUR OWN . . .

WE ARE BUILDING SANDCASTLES ON

THE SHORES OF TIME,

WHICH THE WAVES OF HISTORY

WILL ULTIMATELY WASH AWAY.

God made us for a remarkably intimate relationship with himself, and it is a working relationship. The world God created is headed for destruction, and his deep desire is to save it. He is the-God-Who-Saves, but he does not work alone. He has called us to participate in that saving process. The Father redeems us ^(Put right) through the atonement of the Son and through the quickening work of the Spirit. Then he calls us to join with him in his redemptive work. We are not to work *for* him, but *with* him. *The reason is because there is nothing redemptive in us.* Only as God is present in us and works through us can our work count eternally. So if our work is to be significant, it must be work God does *in* us and *through* us. (As someone has said, the truth of theology is all in the prepositions!) His presence *in* our lives is the basis for anything significant.

The nature of personhood is the key to understanding his presence in our lives and our freedom to work *with* him. People are never individually autonomous. They come *from*, live *in*, and exist *for* and *through* others. Charles Williams writes:

> At the beginning of life in the natural order is an act of substitution and co-inherence. A man can have no child unless his seed is received and carried by a woman; a woman can have no child unless she receives and carries the seed of a man—literally bearing the burden. It is not only a mutual act; it is a mutual act of substitution. The child itself for nine months literally co-inheres in its mother; there is no human creature that has not sprung from such a period of interior growth.[1]

This principle of *co-inherence* is illustrated repeatedly in Scripture and in our everyday lives. The well-being of every human person lies in another. We saw it in the story of Abraham, Isaac, and Sodom and Gomorrah. We saw it in the story of the janitor from Chicago. I did not introduce the subject of God and prayer to him; God was already at work in his life before I met him. So our business in God's kingdom is to find out what God is doing to redeem this world and join him in that work. If we work on our own—even if our work is quite religious and even if it is done ostensibly in the name of Christ—we are building sandcastles on the shores of time, which the waves of history will ultimately wash away.

People are social beings, so the key to understanding a person lies in understanding that person's relationships. We see this in Jesus' insistence that the only way the world can know the Father from whom we all came is through the Son. No one can know God except through Jesus.

Matthew 11 is a poignant account from the life of Jesus. He has just received a delegation from John the Baptist asking if he is really the one John the Baptist announced him to be. Is he really the Christ? Jesus is deeply moved. He first calls attention to his incredible miracle

---

1. Charles Williams, *The Descent of the Dove* (New York: Oxford University Press, 1939), 234.

ministry, which no mere human prophet could have performed. Then he launches into a passionate endorsement of the greatness of John the Baptist himself and chides his own people for rejecting him. This makes Jesus conscious of the fact that he, too, is being rejected. So he speaks about himself. Notice his words. The passage merits close study:

> I thank you, Father, Lord of heaven and earth, because you have hidden these things from the wise and the intelligent and have revealed them to infants; yes, Father, for such was your gracious will. All things have been handed over to me by my Father; and no one knows the Son except the Father, and no one knows the Father except the Son and anyone to whom the Son chooses to reveal him. (Matt 11:25–27 NRSV)

If not to the leadership of Israel, it is quite clear to spiritual "infants": Jesus stands in a unique position between the Father and his world. If we are to know our heavenly Father, there is only one way. It is through Jesus.

Consider Jesus' conversation with his disciples in the upper room on Thursday night before the cross (John 14) in which Jesus explains that he is going to leave them. He is going, he says, to his Father. Note that he does not mention the *place* to which he is going but rather the *person*. Thomas wants to go with him and asks the way. Then Jesus gives his formidable declaration: "I am the way and the truth and the life" (v 6). But he adds these crucial words: "No one comes to the Father except through me. If you really knew me, you would know my Father as well" (vv 6–7). Trying to fully grasp what Jesus is saying, Philip asks him to help them to see the Father. Jesus' response is memorable:

> Have I been with you all this time, Philip, and you still do not know me? Whoever has seen me has seen the Father. How can you say, 'Show us the Father'? Do you not believe that I am in the Father and the Father is in me? The words that I say to you I do not speak on my own, but the Father who dwells in me does

his works. Believe me that I am in the Father and the Father is in me; but if you do not, then believe me because of the works themselves. (John 14:8–11 NRSV)

Jesus understood himself as the bridge, in knowledge and experience, between the Father and the world. To understand the Father, we must understand the Son. To know the Father, we must know the Son. The divine Son is the-One-in-Between.

## Our Mediatorial Role

John's Gospel is based on an understanding of personhood that we, with our modern individualism, have not grasped. John assumes the co-inherence and *interpenetrability* of personhood. We do not have language adequate to express this, but it is what Jesus is speaking about when he prays for the Father to make his disciples one. Note his words as he prays for you and me, as much as for the first disciples who were with him that night:

My prayer is not for them alone. I pray also for those who will believe in me through their message, that all of them may be one, Father, just as you are in me and I am in you. May they also be in us so that the world may believe that you have sent me. (John 17:20–21)

We are back to studying our prepositions, aren't we? God comes in someone else *to* us, and he comes *through* someone else to us. Paul understood this mediatorial relationship. Note his word to the young Timothy in 1 Timothy 2:5–7:

For there is one God and one mediator between God and men, the man Christ Jesus, who gave himself as a ransom for all men— the testimony given in its proper time. And for this purpose I was appointed a herald and an apostle—I am telling the truth, I am not lying—and a teacher of the true faith to the Gentiles.

Clearly, Paul sees both the ministry of Christ and his own ministry mediatorially; both are "stand-between" persons. Christ stands between the Father and Paul, while Paul stands between Christ and the Gentiles. It is difficult for today's readers to understand what Jesus meant when he spoke of himself as the way, but not because his words are unclear. They are crystal clear. He used the same kind of language when he sent his disciples out to preach.

When Jesus sent the Twelve out to preach, teach, and heal, he said many people would not welcome them or their words. He added, "He who receives you receives me, and he who receives me receives the one who sent me" (Matt 10:40). In other words, the Twelve would become the means through which others might receive Christ. In fact, Jesus said that if people rejected the disciples and their words, they were actually rejecting him; and in rejecting him, they were also rejecting the Father, because the Father could be received only through him.

I read that passage a number of times across the years. Oddly, I was in mid-career before the seriousness of that text began to hit me. I did not see the truth contained in these words because I did not expect redemption to work this way. I did not realize that Christ was so closely identified with me and I was so identified with him that whatever people did with me and my preaching, they did with Christ. I frankly did not want that responsibility. I did not want that burden. The idea seemed almost blasphemous. So I thought with gratitude, *Thank God I was not one of the Twelve!*

Then I read Luke 10:16, where Jesus spoke to seventy disciples he was sending out. His message was stated negatively, but in essence it was the same as what he said to the Twelve: "He who listens to you listens to me; he who rejects you rejects me; but he who rejects me rejects him who sent me." Notice that he added, "All things have been committed to me by my Father. No one knows who the Son is except the Father, and no one knows who the Father is except the Son and those to whom the Son chooses to reveal him" (v 22). It seemed obvious that Jesus believed the Father, the Son, and those who believe in the Son are one, so that what you do with one, you do with the others. Again, my reaction was hesitant. What a responsibility! Preaching becomes a different task if one really believes this. Should I try to excuse myself with the fact that I was not one of the seventy?

Then I read John 12–13. The scene here is Jerusalem, during that last week of Christ's life before the cross. Jesus had washed the feet of the disciples in the upper room. In the intimacy of those moments, he spoke to them about their relationship with him and with the Father who had sent him. He wanted them to understand how all of this intersected. So he pronounced what he obviously meant to be understood as a general principle: "I tell you the truth, *whoever* accepts *anyone* I send accepts me; and whoever accepts me accepts the one who sent me" (John 13:20, emphasis added).

Reading this passage, I realized with startling suddenness the full impact of Jesus' words on Easter Sunday evening, which appear several chapters later. Then he spoke to the Twelve, to the women who had gone to care for his body, and to the other men and children who had come together to mourn his death. To protect themselves, they had locked the doors to their room when the risen Jesus suddenly stood in their midst. He said, "Peace be with you" (John 20:19). He showed them his hands and his side to let them know that it was really him. Then he said, "As the Father has sent me, I am sending *you*" (John 20:21, emphasis added). He breathed on them and said, "Receive the Holy Spirit. If you forgive anyone his sins, they are forgiven; if you do not forgive them, they are not forgiven" (vv 22–23).

Every word Jesus spoke that night was loaded with associations that evoked precious memories for those in the room. His reference to the Holy Spirit must have transported several of those disciples back to the Jordan River, where they had seen Jesus baptized and the Spirit descending upon him to prepare him for ministry. Jesus' use of the simple word *sent* must have triggered a veritable flood of memories. It was Jesus' favorite word to describe his relationship to his Father. Over forty times, the two Greek words for *send* are found in the text of the Gospel of John. Jesus said the Father had sent him into the world. On more than one occasion in John's account, Jesus describes his Father with a Greek phrase that literally reads "the-sending-me-Father." Now Jesus is *sending* these who had come to believe in him. Through them, God's forgiveness will be made available to the world. Christ invited his spiritual children into his divine relationship with the Father and the Spirit, so they were now a part of the family business. What he had started, they now were to finish. As the knowledge of God had come to them through the Son, now the knowledge of God was to be spread throughout the world, through them and through others who would believe on him.

## Unbroken Abiding: The Way of Mediation

The mediatorial principle permeates the world of God and man. God comes to us through Christ. Christ and the Father come to the world through those who have faith in Christ. Jesus develops another aspect of the mediatorial principle in his conversation with his disciples in the upper room the night before the cross. He says that anyone who believes in him should have fruit in his or her life as a result. But he is careful to explain that the fruit is not produced by us; rather, it is the result of his divine life within us, so it is actually his fruit. The image he uses is that of the vine and the branches. Note what he says:

> I am the true vine, and my Father is the gardener. He cuts off every branch in me that bears no fruit, while every branch that does bear fruit he prunes so that it will be even more fruitful. You are already clean because of the word I have spoken to you. Remain in me, and I will remain in you. No branch can bear fruit by itself; it must remain in the vine. Neither can you bear fruit unless you remain in me.
>
> I am the vine; you are the branches. If a man remains in me and I in him, he will bear much fruit; apart from me you can do nothing. If anyone does not remain in me, he is like a branch that is thrown away and withers; such branches are picked up,

thrown into the fire and burned. If you remain in me and my words remain in you, ask whatever you wish, and it will be given you. This is to my Father's glory, that you bear much fruit, showing yourselves to be my disciples. (John 15:1–8)

Here Jesus depicts a relationship in which we know no separation from him. It is a relationship in which we abide in him and draw our life from him. As sap flows from a vine into its branches, Christ's life flows into us so that we can live in his strength and empowerment. Jesus insisted that he could do nothing apart from his Father. This is the life he wants us to know, a life in which prayer is not an occasional activity but a continual state of conscious relationship. Christ is *with* us and *in* us, just as we are *in* him. This kind of unbroken life, Jesus says, will inevitably be fruitful. As he says, "If a man remains in me he will bear much fruit. Apart from me you can do nothing." The key to fruitfulness then is to live in him. This unity of life characterized his own relationship with his Father (John 5:30).

He prayed that such a life in us would cause the world to know that the Father had sent him (John 17:21). The life lived in Christ—allowing him to flow out to others—has a power and fruitfulness nothing else has. Corrie ten Boom records a remarkable example of this.

Corrie and her family lived in the Netherlands during the Second World War when Germany occupied the Netherlands. As the Nazis began seeking out Jews so they could destroy them, Corrie and her family actively tried to protect and save some of these Jews. The Nazis discovered their involvement and placed Corrie, her sister, and her father in Ravensbrück concentration camp. Their story is recorded in Corrie's little volume titled *The Hiding Place*.

During their time in the concentration camp, both her sister and her father died. Corrie survived. After the war was over, God gave her a remarkable ministry of witness to God's goodness and love. One day in Munich, she had just finished speaking on the power of Christ to forgive. She was greeting a number of people after her message when suddenly she became conscious of a certain man waiting in line to shake her hand. He was beaming from ear to ear as he approached her. Corrie imagined herself back in the prison camp at Ravensbrück. She was in the room where guards herded the women to take their showers. She could smell the stench, feel her own nudity, but especially see the face of a guard as he leered at her and her sister in their nakedness. The man now standing in front of her was that guard.

She heard him thank her for her message, rejoicing that God had forgiven his sins. Corrie saw his extended hand, but she found no power to lift hers to meet it. She found herself praying, "Lord, I cannot forgive him. Give me *your* forgiveness." Suddenly, she felt a hot surge like fire run down her arm and through her hand. She was able to extend it to meet the hand of that former guard. Instantly, the love of God for that man filled her heart, a love that almost overwhelmed her.

When Christ lives in us without hindrance, and when we live in him, he enables us to do things that can be explained only in this way: Christ is reaching the world through us.

→ Reminds me of story of forgiving Dan & telling him I was sorry & the supernatural puff of air that entered a part of my heart that had atrophied. Like a balloon that had deflated & each side of the latex stuck to the other & it couldn't be blown up again then the Holy Spirit puffed air into that area of my heart that was dead due to my prideful, self righteous stance. When I asked for forgiveness from Dan — the healing came instantly — Praise God! TO HIM be the glory.
Unforgiveness is a sin that blocks

God from me & in me

# 3

## THE CONTEXT OF PRAYER

### AS WE OPEN OUR HEARTS TO GOD,
### HE BEGINS TO SHARE THE BURDENS HE CARRIES.

*Close relationship*

Because we are made in the image of God, we are supposed to "walk with God" as Abraham did. As we do, we find that God himself teaches us how to pray; he opens unknown worlds to our hearts. He exposes our minds to new ideas. He teaches us how to talk with him in the quiet of the day, and he teaches us how to meet him in the press of life. He teaches us the solace of his presence in sorrow and pain, and he shows us the power of his presence in times of need. As we open our hearts to God, he begins to share with us the burdens he carries. He expands our hearts and minds so that we can carry those burdens with him. We find ourselves carrying others' needs in our own hearts, much like a pregnant woman carries a baby in her womb. That is the way God carries his world with its needs in himself. Intimate communion with the triune God opens up vistas of life that we otherwise would never know or dream possible.

George Herbert, a seventeenth-century poet and preacher, wrote a poem that describes some of the wonder of prayer:

> PRAYER the Churches banquet, Angels age,
> Gods breath in man returning to his birth,
> The soul in paraphrase, heart in pilgrimage,
> The Christian plummet sounding heav'n and earth;
> . . . . . .

Softnesse, and peace, and joy, and love, and blisse,
Exalted Manna, gladnesse of the best,
Heaven in ordinarie, man well drest,
The milkie way, the bird of Paradise,
Church-bels beyond the stars heard, the souls bloud,
The land of spices, something understood.[1]

## WHO CAN PRAY? AND WHERE?

At this point, we should ask some basic questions about prayer.
Who is supposed to pray? Where should we pray? For whom should
we pray? How should we pray? A passage from Paul's first letter to
Timothy illuminates all of these questions. Note Paul's admonition
to his young friend and colleague:

> I urge, then, first of all, that requests, prayers, intercession and
> thanksgiving be made for everyone—for kings and all those in
> authority, that we may live peaceful and quiet lives in all godliness
> and holiness. This is good, and pleases God our Savior, who wants
> all men to be saved and to come to a knowledge of the truth. For
> there is one God and one mediator between God and men, the
> man Christ Jesus, who gave himself as a ransom for all men—the
> testimony given in its proper time. And for this purpose I was ap-
> pointed a herald and an apostle—I am telling the truth, I am not
> lying—and a teacher of the true faith to the Gentiles.
>
> I want men everywhere to lift up holy hands in prayer, with-
> out anger or disputing. (1 Tim 2:1–8)

Paul indicates his concern that everyone should pray. Prayer
is not for a select few, but for all. God hears anyone who prays because all people, believers and unbelievers, are objects of God's love.
God longs for all to be saved. That is the reason God took human

---

1. George Herbert, *The Poetical Works of George Herbert* (New York: D. Appleton
and Co., 1857), 61–62.

form as Jesus Christ. From Paul's perspective, prayer is part of God's master design that brought Christ into the world to redeem it, so prayer is crucial to the completion of that design. We are to pray for the political authorities who rule over us. Social chaos is not only damaging to individuals but destructive to the purposes of God. The Roman emperor may have been a pagan, but he maintained conditions of peace across the empire that permitted the apostle Paul to travel and witness as he did. So the emperor's welfare was important to Paul. The emperor enabled him to fulfill his divine calling. The apostle did not hesitate to urge all Christians to pray for the government that maintained such peace. He clearly seems to believe that such prayer actually made a difference. For Paul, the prayers of God's people had a political as well as a spiritual aspect. So he commends all people everywhere to pray. He believes that no prayers are wasted, particularly if they come from those with clean hands and pure hearts filled with love.

I am intrigued by the fact that Paul urges *all* people to pray. He knows that it is natural for human beings to pray, whether we are very religious or not. Robert Jenson has called us "the animals that pray." To be human means to pray sometime, somewhere. It is hard for us not to pray, whether or not we admit it.

That was the experience of a classmate of mine in college who later became a lawyer. We were on a debate team together for three years and got to know each other and our stories quite well. He came from a devout Quaker background, but somehow he turned away from his faith and became agnostic, perhaps even atheistic. He was in some of the worst of the fighting of the Second World War, though afterward he told me with pride that he never prayed during that ordeal. However, after the war, he was driving in eastern Pennsylvania one night and stopped to pick up a hitchhiker. Instead of getting in the front seat with my friend, the stranger opened the back door and got in. Then, my friend said, "I prayed."

The apostle Paul understood this tendency to look for help in moments of crisis, but he did not try to discourage it, no matter how selfish the prayer might be. He knew that such prayers acknowledge that we are not complete in ourselves or in total control of our circumstances. We admit, at least for the moment, that we need help from beyond ourselves.

For Christians, however, prayer means much more. Christians know to whom they pray and they know a great deal about the character of the One to whom they pray. God's very nature and personhood invite prayer. Christians know he is not some distant impersonal force or capricious sprite to be manipulated for one's own ends. He is *personal*; one God in three *persons*, Father, Son, and Spirit. Other-oriented love binds the three divine persons together. Christians find themselves objects of that love and find that God is waiting to hear their prayers. His nature is not capricious but faithful. There is no fluctuation in his love, for love is his essential nature. He is ever open to our prayers. He is everywhere. We do not go to a certain place to present our prayers, for he is already with us. We simply turn our attention to him and acknowledge the prior reality that he has been there all along. This means we can be in communion with him all the time. Thus, Paul could tell Timothy that the Christian believer should pray "everywhere" and "always." He urged the Thessalonian church to pray "without ceasing" (1 Thess 5:17 NRSV). We do not need a sacred place or a sacred time to pray, though sacred spaces and times are not to be despised. God is ready anywhere and always to listen to his children. And his children do pray.

One cannot read the Scriptures without noticing how much the biblical story turns on prayer. The great men and women whose life stories are told in Scripture were people of prayer. A study of their prayers and the divine answers to those prayers will warm any believer's heart. Whatever the problem, whenever and wherever these biblical heroes had a need, prayer was their natural response. It should be the same for us.

## How Should We Pray?

For many people, religion is the worship of spirits in an invisible world. In classical paganism, it was the worship of personified forces of nature that one hoped to manipulate to one's advantage. That is why the thought of appeasement, manipulation, or resignation—so alien to Christian thinking—is such a part of the non-Christian religious mind. The God to whom we Christians pray is no enigmatic, distant stranger. He has revealed himself in Jesus Christ, who insisted that when we see him, we see all there is of God to see. In other words, Christ is a faithful revelation of the One who created us and all other things, the One who loves us enough that he came to us when we could not go to him. Jesus came, not only that we might know what God is like, but also that we might have a personal relationship with him. We do not pray to a "higher power" but to a "very present help" (Ps 46:1 NRSV), whom we address with a personal name. This relationship is personal in a way that no other religion knows.

The reason is the Christian doctrine of the Trinity, which describes a God in whose oneness there are different personal identities—the Father, the Son, and the Holy Spirit. This means that the inner life of the triune Godhead is an interpersonal life of mutual self-giving and receiving. God has invited us to be a part of that interpersonal life. We have been made *by* Someone and *for* Someone, and he has told us his name. Little wonder that we pray in the name of Jesus. It is the name above all names because it gives us access to God.

However, this does not mean that God ignores the prayer of a person who does not know his name. His love is universal. Amy Carmichael, the British missionary to India who had a ministry of redemption with the Hindu temple girls, tells the story of a child named Mimosa. Mimosa found herself in the Dohnavur Fellowship, the community established by Amy Carmichael, where she heard the story of a God who loved her. Her family, unhappy that she was in a Christian school, came and took her away. Mimosa's stay was so brief that she did not even learn the name of Jesus before she was taken away, yet she could not forget the story of a God who loved her. So she prayed to the One whose name she did not know. She began to sense that this God heard her and was responding to her prayers. In due time, he enabled her to return to Dohnavur with great joy. In the company of fellow Christians, Mimosa learned the name of the One she had come to love—Jesus. God undoubtedly hears the prayer of anyone who responds to the overtures of the Spirit of God, the Spirit that seeks all people. In knowing his name, our questions and our uncertainties become confidence and joy.

Since our relationship to God is a personal one, some principles that apply to all personal relationships also apply here. For example, if there is to be any real communication between two people, they must be open to each other. If openness is not there, we simply talk at or past each other. This is as true in our relationship with God as it is in our human relationships.

W. H. Auden gives us a remarkable description of such openness in his comments on his friendship with Charles Williams. Auden said that he counted that friendship

> among my most unforgettable and precious experiences. I have met great and good men in whose presence one was conscious of one's own littleness; Charles Williams' effect on me and on others with whom I have spoken was quite different: in his company one felt twice as intelligent and infinitely nicer than, out of it, one knew oneself to be. It wasn't simply that he was a sympathetic listener—he talked a lot and he talked well—but, more than anyone else I have ever known, he gave himself completely to the company that he was in. So many conversations, even good ones, are really several monologues which only now and then and by accident relate to each other, for the talkers are more concerned with their own thoughts than with a living exchange of ideas, but any conversation with Charles Williams, no matter how trivial or impersonal the topic, was a genuine dialogue.[2]

*may I be like Charles William's in all my conversations!*

[2]. David Garrett Izzo, *W. H. Auden Encyclopedia* (Jefferson, NC: McFarland & Company, Inc., Publishers, 2004), 275.

Some may feel that it is improper to compare a conversation between two human beings with the prayer of a human being to Almighty God. However, Christian prayer expresses a relationship between persons as well. A classic way of explaining this is that we pray to the Father through the Son and at the urging and with the help of the Holy Spirit. Jesus is the God-man who has been where we are and knows all about our sin, our weakness, and our needs. He is different from us to be sure, but he is like us too. When he ascended into heaven, he did not cease to be a human person. Remember the words of John in 1 John 3:1–2:

> How great is the love the Father has lavished on us, that we should be called children of God! And that is what we are! The reason the world does not know us is that it did not know him. Dear friends, now we are the children of God, and what we will be has not yet been made known. But we know that when he appears, we shall be like him, for we shall see him as he is.

Personal communication also depends on *trust*. When we play games with each other or hide from one another, our relationship is broken and communication is blocked. That is why humility is absolutely essential in our relationship to God, a humility that expresses itself in repentance.

Jesus illustrates this in his story of the publican and the Pharisee, found in Luke 18:9–14:

> The Pharisee stood up and prayed about himself: "God, I thank you that I am not like other men—robbers, evildoers, adulterers—or even like this tax collector. I fast twice a week and give a tenth of all I get." But the tax collector stood at a distance. He would not even look up to heaven, but beat his breast and said, "God, have mercy on me, a sinner."

The Pharisee presented himself to God the way he wanted God to see him. The publican presented himself to God just the way he was. He made no attempt to hide his faults from God, but opened himself to him. The very love and life of God flowed into him in forgiveness and new life. The Pharisee presented a barrier of pretense that prevented the love and life of God from flowing into him. His prayer was really a monologue. Significantly, the Greek text actually says that he prayed "to himself." He refused to open himself to God and let himself be known by God. He could not know God because he tried to prevent God from knowing him. On the other hand, the publican went home justified.

Something else must be said about the openness of prayer. It is an evidence of faith. It is difficult to be honest with another if you do not trust that person. Only as we trust God do we open ourselves so that the life of God flows into us. Faith is the necessary condition for the openness and honesty that lead to repentance. We repent only when we have decided that we can and must be honest with God. We must believe that he is trustworthy and that it is safe to open ourselves to him.

At least ten different verbs are used in the New Testament for prayer, yet no special terminology must be used for our prayers to be heard. In the Gospel of John, the expressions Jesus uses in his conversations with the Father are the same as those he uses in conversations with his disciples and others. He apparently had no special phrases that he used when he was talking with his Father. John introduces the most important prayer in the Bible, often called the "high priestly prayer" (John 17), by stating that Jesus "lifted up his eyes to heaven and *said*, 'Father, the hour has come'" (KJV). The New International Version translates this, "He looked toward heaven and *prayed* . . ." The text here uses the common Greek word used just for speaking. So the same word used to denote his speaking to his disciples also signifies his conversations with his heavenly Father.

Since prayer expresses a personal relationship, it may take many forms. The Scriptures describe prayers of petition, praise, thanksgiving, adoration, and intercession. Throughout the Bible, we find prayers offered in moments of aspiration, wonder, persecution, and guilt. At the key moments in life, God's people prayed. God's answers to these prayers became the record of the acts of God in human history.

## WHERE SHOULD WE PRAY?

As we said above, people should be free to pray any time, under any circumstances, and anywhere. Jesus often lifted his heart to his Father in the midst of a conversation with other people and interjected prayer into the midst of human dialogue. John 12:20–32 records how Philip and Andrew go to Jesus to tell him that there are some Greeks at the Passover festival who want to see him. Undoubtedly, their mention of the Greeks reminds him of his approaching death for the whole world. So Jesus speaks to them about the cross, and he suddenly breaks into a conversation with his Father. Those standing nearby think they hear thunder. John tells us that the sound was the very voice of his Father responding to Jesus' prayer (v 29). Since he was never out of the presence of his Father, his Father was a participant in every conversation Jesus had, whether the other people with whom Jesus was talking realized it. Therefore, it was perfectly appropriate for him to address his Father in the course of his conversation.

It has been my privilege to have known some people like that. They could move from a conversation with another person to a conversation with Christ without any transition. For them, the line between this world and that world was so thin that they could cross it with an ease as natural as breathing. If Christ is with us and in us, why not include him in our ordinary conversational life? Jesus included his Father that way.

# 4

# Sin: Disrupting the Conversation

Even Christian religiosity does
not usher us into Christ's kingdom.
That privilege comes with knowing God.

True prayer is no monologue. It is not talking at God; it is talking with him, and we must be willing to listen if we wish to be heard.

As we have said elsewhere, Scripture describes the relationship of a believer with God by using the familial metaphors of a child's relationship with a father and a spouse's relationship with a mate. True, the Scriptures also use legal metaphors to describe this relationship; however, they do not adequately express the intimacy God obviously seeks with us. The courtroom is a place for pronouncements, not intimate conversations. The family hearth and the marriage bed have a much different ambience. These familial settings are characterized by intimacy based on mutual commitment, trust, and love. These qualities cannot exist where conversational partners are not open with one another. That is the problem with sin: It inevitably puts fear, distrust, and distance between God and us so that we close ourselves off from him and others.

The first biblical picture of this disrupted relationship is in the garden of Eden. When Adam and Eve sinned, they immediately were afraid to trust God and began to distrust each other. They fled from meeting with God. The relationship of openness, trust, and love was lost. Sin always brings separation from the saving God and from other creatures. And to be separated from God means to be lost, because he is our salvation.

Unfortunately, today much Christian teaching and preaching focuses solely on helping people to be saved—to find forgiveness or to inherit eternal life, as if this were enough. The question of an individual's eternal destiny seems paramount, and the protection of oneself is the prime concern. However, this emphasis can separate the truth of salvation from Jesus himself. Salvation is not a *thing* that we can possess for our personal advantage. Salvation is the personal transformation that occurs when the Savior, Jesus, comes into our lives. There is no salvation apart from his abiding presence, for he alone is the Savior. Jesus spoke quite clearly about this on the night before his crucifixion. In his prayer to the heavenly Father, which is the culmination of his teaching ministry to his disciples, he described salvation this way:

> Father, the time has come. Glorify your Son, that your Son may glorify you. For you granted him authority over all people that he might give eternal life to all those you have given him. Now this is eternal life: that they may know you, the only true God, and Jesus Christ, whom you have sent. (John 17:1–3)

The message seems clear enough, but the apostle Paul adds another detail. He says that salvation is *being known by* God as well as knowing God. In his Galatian letter, Paul writes to people who have come to saving faith under his teaching but are now turning away from Christ. He reminds them of the difference Christ has made in their lives:

> Formerly, when you did not know God, you were slaves to those who by nature were not gods. But now that you know God—*or rather are known by God*—how is it that you are turning back to those weak and miserable principles? Do you wish to be enslaved by them all over again? (Gal 4:8–9, emphasis added)

Paul is making explicit what was implied in Jesus' words: Personal knowledge must be reciprocal. God does not know some people because they will not be open to him, and there is no salvation apart from the presence of Christ in a person's life. Therefore, when Christians harbor unconfessed and unrepented sin in their lives, they withdraw from God. Prayer in this context is meaningless. In the Sermon on the Mount, Jesus speaks of those who have done remarkable miracles in his name but whom he does not *know* (Matt 7:21–23). Even Christian religiosity does not usher us into Christ's kingdom. That privilege comes with knowing God and being known personally by him.

There is an irony in the story of Adam and Eve we must not miss. When the Serpent was tempting them, he said that if they ate the fruit God had forbidden them to eat, they would not die but would become like God. In other words, the Serpent told them he cared more about their welfare than God did! The irony is that the one thing promised by the Serpent is exactly what they lost by listening to him—the very likeness of God himself.

The Scriptures make clear that the nature of God is to care more about his creatures than he does about himself. He is holy, other-oriented love. That is demonstrated clearly in the incarnation. Jesus further emphasizes it when he speaks of himself as the good shepherd. The supreme characteristic of the good shepherd is that he "lays down his life for his sheep." The well-being of the sheep is his primary motive (John 10:15). And Jesus insists that his Father loves him precisely because he lays down his life for the sheep (John 10:17). Jesus explains this more fully to the Twelve in the upper room just before he goes to the cross:

> As the Father has loved me, so I have loved you; abide in my love. If you keep my commandments, you will abide in my love, just as I have kept my Father's commandments and abide in his love. I have said these things to you so that my joy may be in you, and that your joy may be complete. This is my commandment, that you love one another as I have loved you. No

one has greater love than this, to lay down one's life for one's friends. You are my friends if you do what I command you. I do not call you servants any longer, because the servant does not know what the master is doing; but I have called you friends, because I have made known to you everything that I have heard from my Father. (John 15:9–15 NRSV)

Paul accepts this pattern of Christian life as imaging God. Note his words to the Ephesian believers:

Be imitators of God, therefore, as dearly loved children and live a life of love, just as Christ loved us and gave himself up for us as a fragrant offering and sacrifice to God. (Eph 5:1–2)

God's children were made to image their Father so that when he looked at them he could see a likeness of himself in his family members. The children were to image their Father so faithfully that when they looked at each other, they could see the family resemblance in one another. That family resemblance is seen in agape love, which is being willing to lay down one's life for another. With Eve's and Adam's sin, that divine image was lost. Now the dominating characteristic of God's creatures became self-interest, which was the antithesis of the nature of the One who made, sustained, and would later die for them.

As we said, the ironies in Eden are remarkable. The Serpent promised Eve that if she would do as he suggested, she would become like God. In reality, her likeness to God is what she lost. The thing that was highest, noblest, and best about the two human beings in the garden was that God made them as much like himself as a creature could be, and the supreme mark of God in them was his holy, other-oriented love. The psalmist tells us God made us a little lower than himself (Ps 8:5 NRSV). We are not divine, but almost. That idea was too much for the translators of the Greek Septuagint, so they translated the Hebrew word for God in this passage (*Elohim*) with the Greek word for angels. So the NIV tells us that God made us "a little lower than the heavenly beings." How hard it is for us in our sinfulness to realize how God made us originally! He intended us to be images of himself.

The Serpent told Eve that when she ate the forbidden fruit, her eyes would be opened. Instead, her eyes were blinded. She fell prey to an illusion and no longer saw the reality of creation. She thought the fruit would improve her understanding. But instead of making her wise, it made her foolish enough to trade a loving relationship with God himself for the existential loneliness of a heart separated from the very source of life and all that is holy. Eve's choice was not life but death. Trust in the One who made her became distrust. The other-oriented love that is God himself was replaced by an arrogant selfishness and an existential fear. She traded God's presence within her for the emptiness of an ego lost in itself.

Paul makes this clear in his epistles as he describes two ways of life. One is life in the Spirit; the other is what Paul calls life in the "flesh." This is a major theme in his epistles to the Romans and Galatians particularly. Paul indicates that there is no third choice; there are only two. The way of the "flesh" is the way of life Eve chose. By life in the "flesh," Paul means a life that is centered in oneself rather than in God, from whom life comes. Some of our Bible translations are not helpful here. The NIV translates the Greek word *sarx* (literally "flesh") as "sinful nature." This implies that something alien has been added to us by sin, which corrupts us. The reality is just the opposite. When we human beings sinned, something vital was lost. We shut ourselves off from God, who is the source of all that is holy and good. The loving presence of God, who should be our guide and sustainer, was gone. We were left to ourselves, empty of God. Lesslie Newbigin, India's and Britain's great missionary statesman, gives us a most helpful definition for "flesh" and explains the difference between life in the Spirit and life in the "flesh":

> The words "flesh" and "Spirit" do not refer to parallel and analogous realities in our experience, such as "visible" and "invisible" or "lower nature" and "higher nature." "Flesh" denotes the whole of our creaturely being insofar as it seeks to organize

itself and to exist in its own power and apart from the continually renewed presence and power of God, "from above."[1]

Adam and Eve's problem was that they decided to organize their lives around themselves rather than around the One who is the true center and source of all things, the One who made them and gave them every breath. This reorganization of their lives was sin. Augustine and Luther spoke of this as the "heart curved in upon itself" (*cor incurvatus ad se*). Isaiah described it with the words, "We have turned everyone to his own way" (Isa 53:6 KJV). Self instead of God became central in human life. With the loss of the source of all goodness and love, human history began its long course of corruption and death.

Fortunately, Scripture gives us the story of another human being who lived life differently. In Romans 5 and 1 Corinthians 15 (NRSV), Paul contrasts "the first man, Adam" with "the last Adam, a life-giving spirit." That second man was Christ, who came to undo the damage Adam and Eve brought into our world. Jesus is indeed a striking contrast to Adam and Eve. His life was lived in the Spirit. His very conception in the womb of Mary was an act of the Holy Spirit. The descent of the Spirit upon him, when John the Baptist baptized him, prepared him for his public ministry. He was led immediately by the Spirit into the wilderness, where he was tempted by the same one who tempted Adam and Eve. However, he overcame the deceptions of Satan through the power of the Spirit and the Word of God. His miracles were performed through the Spirit's power. In the power of the Spirit, he found grace to offer himself on Calvary as an acceptable sacrifice for our sins. The writer of the book of Hebrews says it well when he contrasts the sacrifice of Christ with the animal sacrifices of the old Levitical system: "How much more will the blood of Christ, who through the eternal Spirit offered himself without blemish to God, purify our conscience from dead works to worship the living God?" (Heb 9:14 NRSV).

---

1. Lesslie Newbigin, *The Light Has Come: An Exposition of the Fourth Gospel* (Grand Rapids, MI: William B. Eerdmans Company, 1982), 39–40.

Jesus lived in and by the Spirit. Little wonder that when Jesus was leaving his disciples, his most comforting words were that his Father was going to give them the same Holy Spirit (John 14:26).

This is why we need to be very sensitive to the voice of the Spirit. He will check us when we tend to turn to the "flesh." He will prompt us to resist the "flesh" because he came to glorify God and finish the work that began in Christ's own sacrifice. So he will check us at some very tender spots!

During the middle of my academic career, my son was in his upper teens and attempting to find his own way in distinction from his father. During this period of disassociation, he determined to show his independence in ways that seemed to be a deliberate attempt to embarrass me publicly. So I added some urgency to my prayer for God to change my son. Then the Spirit asked me why I was praying so urgently. Suddenly, I realized that I was more concerned about my own reputation than I was about my son. My seemingly righteous prayers were being filtered through a mesh of self-interest. Jesus was not overly concerned about his reputation when he suffered the obloquy of the cross. I knew immediately that my own fear of embarrassment came from a desire to protect my ego. My concern for my son was corrupted by the concern for what people would think of me. The Spirit led me to realize that this was hindering my prayers. Eventually, I found myself praying, "Lord, my reputation does not matter. My son is what matters. Forgive me and cleanse my heart." I have never regretted that prayer. It was a means not only of identifying with my son but also with Jesus himself.

## THE SELF-ORIENTED LIFE

Recall Lesslie Newbigin's statement: "'Flesh' denotes the whole of our creaturely being insofar as it seeks to organize itself and to exist in its own power and apart from the continually renewed presence and power of God, 'from above.'"[2] The problem of the sinner is not

2. Ibid., 40.

that something alien has been added to his life, but that something vital has been lost. The absence of God's Spirit, in part or in whole, results in a disintegration of the self. God made us to be filled with his Spirit. So the "flesh," as Paul explains it, is any part of me that is not under the control of the Spirit. When sin is present in my life, the Holy Spirit is absent. The source of the divine is gone. So if I live in the "flesh," I cannot please God. In fact, any part of me that I do not surrender to God carries within it the seeds of death.

The liturgy of the church illustrates this. Take baptism, for instance, whether one believes in sprinkling or immersion. Sprinkling symbolizes the fact that to become a Christian is to be marked by the same Spirit who came upon Jesus at his baptism. That Spirit comes upon us and becomes the integrating force in our lives. Jesus refers to this when he speaks of being "born from above," born of the Spirit. Paul can thus say that "if anyone does not have the Spirit of Christ, he does not belong to Christ" (Rom 8:9). Immersion, as pictured by Paul in Romans 6, reminds us that when we become Christians, we die to sin and are resurrected to a new life in Christ as the Spirit lives within us.

This is why the Scriptures emphasize the importance of a clean heart. My will, if it is not one with God's will, always defiles me and leaves me unclean. That defilement puts an obstacle in my relationship to God and hinders his will from being done in my life. My prayers then lose their power. So the Scriptures speak of the need for an undivided heart, an eye that is "single" (Matt 6:22 KJV). The apostle James says that a double-minded person "should not think he will receive anything from the Lord" (James 1:7–8). He insists that we need pure hearts with a single intention (4:8). Paul expresses his concern to the new Christians in Corinth that, though they have started their Christian walk, they are still "fleshly" (1 Cor 3:3 NASB).[3] David prays, "Create in me a clean heart, O God, and put a new and right spirit within me. Do not cast me away from your presence, and do not take your holy spirit from me" (Ps 51:10–11 NRSV).

---

3. The NIV says "worldly," but the word in the Greek text is the adjectival form of *sarx*, the Greek word for "flesh."

Jesus summed this up with his promise, "Blessed are the pure in heart, for they will see God" (Matt 5:8). A pure heart evidently means a heart that is fully open to God with no pretense. Only such a heart can be filled by God's Spirit. Some people think that such spiritual purity is not possible in this life, but Jesus puts that promise in the midst of the Beatitudes. All of the other Beatitudes are obviously intended for this life; why should this one be an exception?

If you have difficulty accepting the idea of a pure heart, remember that the question is not whether you can cleanse your heart. The question is whether the blood of Christ can wash you clean and whether the Holy Spirit can purge you of all spiritual impurity. (Is that not why the Spirit's baptism is called a "baptism of fire"?) When we permit the Holy Spirit to do this, the freedom is glorious. It is the freedom for which our spirits long, for which we were made. It is the freedom God intends for every person made in his image to enjoy.

A friend had just spoken on this subject when a lady approached, obviously in some agitation. She said, "Do you mean to tell me that God can deliver me from my obsession with myself? Are you saying he can change my self-centeredness so that I can think of somebody other than myself? I am so sick of myself that I do not know what to do!"

She was right: Self-centeredness is a sickness. It is not what God made us for. He made us to be temples for his Spirit. When he lives within us, we are truly capable of loving other people, and our prayers become real dialogue with God.

Baptism symbolizes the surrender of our autonomous self-will. This is what George Mueller meant when he said:

> There was a day when I died, literally died to George Mueller—his opinions, preferences, tastes, and will, died to the world, its approval, to the approval or blame even of my brethren and friends—and since then I have studied only to show myself approved unto God.[4]

4. A. T. Pierson, *George Mueller of Bristol* (Old Tappan, NJ: Fleming H. Revell Company, 1899).

The result of that death was new life. George Mueller's life of prayer became one of the most remarkable stories in the history of the Christian church. It is easy to see the secret of Mueller's prayers: his will had become one with God's, and his life was filled with Christ. Mueller spoke of it as a kind of death because it was the end of the tyranny of self-interest. What he found was a new way of living, in the Spirit and not in the "flesh."

## LIFE ORIENTED AROUND JESUS

A final word of clarification: When we speak about this crucifixion of self, we do not mean the destruction of the self, any more than the crucifixion of Jesus was the end of Jesus. God does not destroy people. He seeks their fulfillment. However, our fulfillment is never found in ourselves; it is found in him. We find fulfillment when we are entirely under his control. God simply wants us to find the fullness of life for which he made us. What is cleansed away is the self-will that resists the will of God, the self-centeredness that defiles us and is so unlike the spirit of Jesus.

Self-interest is always obnoxious when we see it in others. We may not see it in ourselves until the Holy Spirit reveals it. Until then, we may think it is "just natural." Yet the original purpose of God for us was a clean heart, not a carnal heart. We must allow the Holy Spirit to remove the screen of self-interest so that we can pray wisely, without greed or ulterior motives or selfish agendas. God does not normally answer selfish prayers, because that would abet our destructiveness. When our hearts are spiritually clean, we can pray, "Not my will, but thine, be done" (cf. Luke 22:42 KJV). Then we know that God's will is entirely good for us. God's will alone is what we need and what others need in us. A clean heart makes us open to God for the sake of that relationship itself, but also for the sake of others, whose needs he wants us to bear in our hearts.

# 5

## PRAYING WITH FREEDOM

### GOD'S COMMANDS ARE NOT BURDENS BUT INVITATIONS TO FREEDOM.

The heavenly Father's love is a life-affirming, all-encompassing love in which we can be truly free. When we love others that way and pray for them with that kind of love, they have a freedom to respond to us and to God in a way that is impossible if our prayers are selfish. So Jesus says to his disciples,

> As the Father has loved me, so have I loved you. Now remain in my love. If you obey my commands, you will remain in my love, just as I have obeyed my Father's commands and remain in his love. I have told you this so that my joy may be in you and that your joy may be complete. My command is this: Love each other as I have loved you. (John 15:9–12)

Christ commands me to love others the way he loves me. Is that an impossible command? At this point, I am extremely grateful to John Wesley, who said that God's commands are really implicit promises. If God tells me to have a pure heart, it is because he has the power to purify my heart. If he tells me to live above conscious sin, it means he can keep me there; he will enable me not to sin. His commands are promises that he will do in me all that I need him to do. His commands are not burdens, but invitations to freedom. When he delivers me from my own limitations, the effects of that freedom ripple across the lives of those I know and love.

For a number of years, I served on the board of a national organization that included representatives of all the major Christian denominations in the country. In those meetings, I occasionally sat next to a board member who was the director of evangelism for his denomination in one of our largest states. I enjoyed his company. So when I attended the meetings, I looked for him and hoped that I could enjoy his fellowship. After one of these semi-annual meetings, I found that his gate at the airport was across from my gate. Both of us had some time before our flights, so we sat down together to talk. He said, "Kinlaw, let me tell you a story."

He described how he had become a Christian and sensed that God wanted him in the ministry. He completed his training, and in his early thirties, he found himself in a demanding pastorate. He had a fairly large staff to assist him in his work, and he was successful in the eyes of his peers, but a deep sense of frustration gnawed at him. He even considered leaving the ministry. One day, he went into his study and threw himself prostrate on the floor. He prayed, "Lord, if this is all there is to the ministry, it is not worth it."

As he lay there, a remarkable sense of the presence of the Lord came over him. Let me use his own language to describe it: "It was as if I were a briefcase. God picked me up, turned me upside down, and began to shake me." He was shocked when he began to see the things that tumbled out of his soul: unclean things that he knew were not pleasing to God and obviously had to go.

He said, "Then it was as if God turned me right side up and filled me with himself. A glorious light filled the room and an unbelievable joy came to me as I sensed the cleanness inside." However, he decided not to tell anyone what had happened.

A few weeks later, he was in a staff meeting. When they finished their stated agenda, the staff turned their eyes to one of the group and sat still, as if they were waiting for that person to do something. The staff member said, "Pastor, we have noticed that something has happened to you, and we like the change. If something *has* happened, could you tell us about it? We would like to know what's going on." Soon afterward, he had a similar experience with his board of trustees.

When God changes our hearts, we like it—and other people do too.

We live in a day when Christian leaders emphasize the power of the Holy Spirit, without mentioning how the Spirit can give us a clean heart, an unmixed motive, and a pure love. We seek the Spirit for his gifts, but not so that he can have his way in us. As a result, all sorts of religious groups in our society do not give a pure witness for Christ; consequently, the outside world is suspicious of our Christian egotism, evidenced by our selfish prayers and lives. The secret to genuine prayer, which is the secret of Christian living, is purity of heart and intention. Prayer has no power unless we are spiritually pure. Purity of heart and life must precede the life of prayer. If our prayers are to have real impact in our world, we must first allow God's Spirit to cleanse us and set us free.

When I was a postgraduate student at Princeton, our chapel service normally consisted of a hymn, a Scripture reading, a prayer, a closing hymn, and a benediction. We followed that formula every week, so the only unique thing about a service was the prayer. A philosophy professor occasionally led our chapel service. When he did, the attendance was larger than on other days, because students wanted to hear him pray. He always began his prayer, "Our living Lord . . . " Something about this man and his reverent words made us feel that we were in the divine presence. I studied under that professor and came to know him personally. What he appeared to be in chapel, he was in private. The agape love of God flowed through him. Behind the words of his public prayer were a life of genuine holiness and a remarkable devotion to Christ.

What gives a Christian that kind of power in prayer? Purity of heart and purpose, and these come from the cleansing presence of the Holy Spirit controlling one's heart.

Jesus supremely manifested his agape love for us in his passion. John describes this love in his first epistle. Agape enables one to lay down one's life for another. John says, "We know love by this, that [Christ] laid down his life for us—and we ought to lay down our lives for one another" (1 John 3:16 NRSV). Jesus tells us that this kind of love, which was in him, is available to us. It is not merely human love at its best. It is a kind of love that can be found only in God. This is why Jesus closed his high priestly prayer on the night before the cross with these words:

> Righteous Father, the world does not know you, but I know you; and these know you that you have sent me. I made your name known to them, and I will make it known, so that the love with which you have loved me may be in them, and I in them. (John 17:25–26 NRSV)

Jesus expects the very love that is in the heart of the Father, divine love, to be in his disciples. The presence of this divine love within us enables the world to identify us as true Christians, because God the Holy One is present only where that love is found. During the same week before his crucifixion, Jesus told his disciples:

> I give you a new commandment, that you love one another. Just as I have loved you, you also should love one another. By this everyone will know that you are my disciples, if you have love for one another. (John 13:34–35 NRSV)

Notice that the love that is supposed to characterize our lives is the very love that binds the three persons of the triune Godhead together. John says this love is actually who God is. It is not bestowed upon us as the result of a decision on the part of God. It is his very nature; it is who he is. So he loves us, not because of who we are, but because of who he is. It is simply an expression of God's nature.

Agape love is not a response to the attractiveness or desirability of the person loved. That is why Christ loved the ungodly (Rom 5:6), even those who were killing him (Luke 23:34). Agape love is what moved Christ to die for the ungodly, to sacrifice himself for us while we were still sinners (Rom 5:5–8). When such love is present in us, we can turn the other cheek and wish well to the person who hates us and despitefully uses us. Paul makes clear that the only source of such love within us is the Spirit of God, who can shed Christ's love abroad in our hearts.

Since agape love originates in God, our human efforts cannot originate it or duplicate it. It is not a consecrated kind of human love. We must receive it from God, and we receive it only by allowing God to enter our lives. It is the indisputable evidence that God lives within us. We may hinder the expression of agape love, but it comes when he comes, because it is who he is. The qualities of agape love are beautifully described in 1 Corinthians 13, which says:

> Love is patient, love is kind. It does not envy, it does not boast, it is not proud. It is not rude, it is not self-seeking, it is not easily angered, it keeps no record of wrongs. Love does not delight in evil but rejoices with the truth. It always protects, always trusts, always hopes, always perseveres. (vv 4–7)

Since this is other-oriented love, I like to paraphrase the passage in a way that emphasizes *others*:

> Love is patient with others and kind to others. It does not envy others. It is not proud and is not rude to others. It is not self-seeking and is not easily angered with others. It does not keep a record of the wrongs of others. It does not rejoice in evil but rejoices with the truth. It always protects others, trusts others, lives in hope, and perseveres.

This scripture underscores the fact that such love can never originate in me. It must come from God. This is why I need him.

How does this love make our lives different? First of all, agape love enables us to live a surrendered life. It gives us a liberty that most of our world does not know. If we are to be intercessors with God, we must settle in our own lives that we are not governed by our own wills but by his will. For God's will to be supreme, Scripture says that our will must be crucified. The way of the cross is the Christian way of life. It is surprising what can be done in human relationships if we bow to others because we have first bowed to Christ.

Early in my life, I read a biography of an Indian man whose name was Sundar Singh. His family was of the Sikh religion, so they were hostile to Christian missionaries and Bible distributors who came to their community. Sundar took part in burning the Bibles of one colporteur who came through his village.

He was hungry for God, though, and he kept seeking God. He wanted to be a Hindu priest, but he did not find peace in his devout Hindu studies. In his disillusionment, he decided one night to lie down across a railroad track near his home to end his life. That night, Christ appeared to him in a dramatic way (much like he appeared to Saul on the road to Damascus) and identified himself as the One described in the Bibles that Sundar had helped to burn. So Sundar began to follow Christ. His family tried to poison him, and he became an outcast. He attached himself to a group of like-minded Christians and committed himself to minister in the villages of northern India, where no Christian had ever gone.

When he entered one village and began to preach Christ, the local leaders said, "If you continue to preach, we will kill you." They put him in a prison cell, stripped him, and then poured a basketful of leeches over his naked body. The leeches fastened themselves to his flesh and began to suck the blood from his body. His tormenters stood around, laughing and saying, "Now you will curse your God and die!"

As they watched him writhe in pain, they noticed that he suddenly relaxed. He looked up and began to lovingly tell them about Jesus. They sensed the passionate love of his heart for them.

Realizing their efforts were futile, they pulled the leeches from his body and let him live.

Then they asked Sundar Singh, "How could you talk to us like that?"

"Well," he said, "when the pain got so intense that I did not think I could bear it, Jesus walked right down the prison corridor and stepped into my heart. His love filled me so that I forgot everything but his love for you and his love for me."

God's agape love, poured into our hearts, frees us to love those who are different from us, reject us, and even persecute us.

## LIVE IN OPENNESS

A second evidence of a heart filled with agape is a willingness to live in openness with God and other people. God's love frees us from having to keep up a defensive front because we find our security in the Lord Jesus. Paul describes it this way: "[Love] does not boast, it is not proud." We are not living in competition with other people; we lovingly give ourselves for them. This is another source of glorious freedom.

One day I received a letter from a pastor who had been in the ministry for ten years. He had come across a reference to Ezekiel 47, which tells of a stream of water flowing out of the temple in Jerusalem, a stream that begins as a trickle but turns into a mighty river. Ezekiel 47 says that the stream turns south to the Dead Sea, where a great transformation takes place. Whereas the Dead Sea is normally clogged with salt and chemical death, the waters of the river in Ezekiel's vision make it fresh and sweet. Ezekiel notices fish swimming in the water that had been deadly sterile before. Grass begins to grow on the banks of the Dead Sea. Where there had been only bitter barrenness, new life breaks forth. Along the banks of the lake, fruit-producing trees begin to grow. Their fruit and leaves are used for the healing of the nations.

This pastor wrote, "At that point, the Spirit said, 'God wants to do something like that in your heart.' I had been digging in the hard clay of my heart, working hard to be fruitful and producing nothing but sterility. So I found myself looking up and saying, 'Lord, let the water flow!'"

He continued, "I really wasn't prepared for what happened. I began to like people! In fact, I enjoyed being with them. I began saying to my wife, 'We must have such-and-such a couple come over.' At first, she did not take me seriously because she knew I was terrified at the thought of having my parishioners visit us. Suddenly, though, I wanted to open our home to them. I even developed a sense of humor. I had always been a stuffy type of person; I couldn't laugh with anybody because I couldn't laugh at myself. But after the Holy Spirit came, I could laugh at my own mistakes and laugh with others. I was free to enjoy my people."

He added, "I also found that I could witness to people outside the church. It is very difficult to tell people about Christ if we believe we need their approval. But the new love within me was so great that I was willing to be vulnerable to the opinions of other people. I was not embarrassed to share with them what a wonderful thing it is to know Christ."

This life of openness is what Jesus was talking about when he stood in the court of the temple in Jerusalem and said:

> "If anyone is thirsty, let him come to me and drink. Whoever believes in me, as the Scripture has said, streams of living water will flow from within him." By this he meant the Spirit whom those who believed him were later to receive. Up to that time the Spirit had not been given, since Jesus had not yet been glorified. (John 7:37–39)

## LIVE IN FORGIVENESS

A further sign of agape love is the freedom to forget the offenses of other people against us. This is why Paul declares that "love keeps no record of wrongs." When you and I have our private time with the Lord Jesus, do we open a little black book where we have recorded the sins or failings of other people? If we do, our prayers will be ineffective. It will not matter how much we pray, because our blighted relationships with those people will hinder our relationship with God.

The grace of Christ can keep our relationships pure, so that when we pray for someone who has harmed us, we genuinely want what would be in their best interest. Only the love of God, poured out in our hearts, can make this possible.

A missionary friend from Colombia shared an unusual experience that illustrated this. One day she heard a knock at the door, and when she opened it, she thought she was facing a man in his fifties. (She later learned he was in his mid-twenties.) He explained that he had killed three missionaries who had been captured by terrorists a few years before. He said, "Now God has forgiven me, and I must get in touch with the wives and families of those people to ask for their forgiveness."

The man told the missionary of the joy the three men had exhibited during their captivity in spite of their circumstances. They kept telling their guards how much Christ loved them and said that they, too, loved them. Their guards could see the missionaries' love for their Bibles, so they took them away, but their joy was undiminished. The missionaries' witness was so impressive that five of their guards became Christians—so those guards were killed.

Finally, this man was ordered to kill the missionaries, and he commanded them to dig their own graves. While they dug, they sang hymns and quoted scriptures to each other and to him. They told him they believed God would save him one day and they would meet him in heaven. After their execution, he became a believer.

Now the converted terrorist knew he must make his confession to their families. He heard that my friend could help him, and indeed she put him in touch with families of the slain missionaries. The mother of one of them later wrote to her:

> We were very moved to receive the confession from the man you worked with . . . My husband is preaching through the Lord's Prayer, and this week he had the section, "Forgive us our debts as we forgive our debtors." He decided to tell the story of our son's death based on the confession we received.

Her husband told their congregation of the terrorist's letter and said that he would forgive the man who killed his son. He explained that God's Holy Spirit had put forgiving love in his heart, so that he could say honestly that he loved this man. For her part, the mother added:

> I freely forgive _____, and the others who kidnapped and held him. I am sincerely rejoicing that several of them have come to know the Lord, and will be again with Mark in glory forever. I think of King David, who had one of his loyal friends killed and robbed his wife. Yet I believe they are together in glory and that Uriah forgave David, and both are rejoicing in God's forgiveness. Someday I hope to meet _____ and others who were with Mark during those very difficult years. We have so very much to thank God for. I am truly thankful for the confirmation that my son was faithful to our dear Lord till the very end. I am also truly thankful that he was used by his dear Savior to testify to others. Thanks so very much. Please convey this message to _____.

With our own best intentions, we would be unable to forgive like this, but God sets us free to respond to others with his own supernatural love and to forgive them with the forgiveness Christ declared on the cross: "Father, forgive them for they do not know what they are doing" (Luke 23:34). The apostle Stephen expressed this kind of forgiveness as he was being stoned to death. He prayed, "Lord, do not hold this sin against them" (Acts 7:60). What is impossible for us apart from God becomes possible when we are filled with him.

## LIVE IN GENEROSITY

Finally, the Holy Spirit can free us to concentrate on meeting the needs of the world because we have entrusted our own needs to God. He can free us to believe he is trustworthy so that we no longer wish for what others have. Then we can live joyfully on meager resources instead of pleading for God to give us more. John Wesley declared that the tenth commandment, "You shall not covet" (Ex 20:17), is actually a promise that God can deliver us from coveting. No person can earnestly pray for the needs of the world if he believes he must have something of this world's goods for himself.

I love C. S. Lewis's words: "He who has God and everything has no more than he who has God alone."[1] If you have Jesus Christ, you will find that he is enough.

Paul tells us that the Holy Spirit will pour out God's love into our hearts, beginning at the new birth (Rom 5:5). The minute you were born again, you began to love others with Christ's agape love, but it is not perfected there. It is perfected only when you let his sanctifying Spirit permeate your spirit. Then your self-will is lost in his will, your way is lost in his way, and his way becomes not a burden but a delight. Johann Franck understood this. Note his prayer:

Jesus, priceless Treasure,
Fount of purest pleasure,
Truest Friend to me.
Ah, how long in anguish
Shall my spirit languish,
Yearning, Lord, for Thee?
Thou art mine, O Lamb divine!
I will suffer naught to hide Thee,
Naught I ask beside Thee.[2]

How free are you? Are you free enough to pray as you should?

1. C. S. Lewis, as quoted in Randy Alcorn, *Money, Possessions and Eternity* (Carol Stream, IL: Tyndale House Publishers, 2003), 15

2. Johann Franck, "Jesus, Priceless Treasure," *Lutheran Hymnal* (St. Louis, MO: Concordia Publishing House, 1941), 347.

# 6

## THE CROSS IN OUR PRAYER LIFE

### THE MAJORITY OF OUR PRAYERS ARE INTENDED TO SERVE OURSELVES.

Wherever we find Christians, the cross symbolizes most clearly what they believe. The cross has always stood at the center of the gospel. I remember when I first became aware of the centrality of the cross in the life of Jesus. I saw that its shadow overcast every part of his life, from his very birth. That shadow became a reality the moment a Roman soldier grasped Jesus' hand to nail it to that rough wood and left him hanging on the cross until he breathed his last. The cross was at the heart of his identity; it was at the heart of his mission; it was at the heart of his ministry; it was at the heart of his prayers. Moreover, the cross was in his Father's heart from the first moment of creation.

Experiencing the cross in prayer is essential for our identification with Jesus. The Holy Spirit brings us to a surrendering so total that the self dies to its self-centeredness and a new creature comes into being. We are set free to love others without the need to control them for our own interests. Consequently, our prayers no longer attempt to manipulate others, as we did without the Holy Spirit's guidance. Before the Holy Spirit comes, our human instinct is to fight for our own survival, so we look for ways to make other people help us live and be happy. Our prayers attempt to control people, situations, and even God for our advantage. Unless we have Spirit-filled hearts, our prayer life becomes increasingly an extension of our self-interest. But when the cross becomes central to our lives, we become free to love others without trying to control them.

It would be interesting to use a tape recorder to capture the prayers of our churches for a year and then go back and analyze what we ask God to do for us. I'm afraid that the majority of our prayers are intended to serve ourselves, like this:

"Lord, would you change this family of mine? Could you straighten them out?"
"My wife is ill. Lord, if you will, take care of her so that she can take care of me."
"Lord, my business is not going well. If you will just help me get through this . . ."

We often pray for the healing of our bodies. God is interested in the health of our bodies, of course, but he is much more interested in the health of our souls. That is where our real sickness lies. How many of our prayers (corporate or private) are for the welfare of our souls or the souls of others? We imagine all the things we want God to give us, and we suppose that if God would give them to us we would be extremely happy. But these are not the kind of prayers Jesus prayed.

## Prayer That Leads to a Surrendered Life

If you give your life to Christ, he will call you to the cross. That doesn't sound pleasant, and let us not gloss over the truth: The cross is a bloody, painful thing. Certainly, Jesus saw it that way. When he was called to the cross, Jesus fell on his face and sweated profusely, as if he were sweating blood. He prayed, "Father, if possible, let this pass from me. I don't want it. But if there is no other way, I will take it" (Luke 22:42, paraphrase). He prayed that prayer three times, yet his heavenly Father did not excuse him from the cross. He told his disciples, "Now my heart is troubled, and what shall I say? 'Father, save me from this hour'? No, it was for this very reason I came to this hour. Father, glorify your name!" (John 12:27–28). The salvation of our world came out of that costly prayer of surrender.

In prayer, Jesus gives the clearest expression of his surrender to the heavenly Father and the Father's will. Here we see a picture of Jesus' full surrender and willingness to accept the cross: "Father, into your hands I commit my spirit" (Luke 23:46). Likewise, our only hope of living a surrendered life is to live in prayer. When we have an ongoing conversation with our Father in prayer, he enables us to surrender to his will.

Do you think Christ has any regrets today about his surrender in Gethsemane? The glory he knows in heaven is the result of what happened on the cross. So let me ask you something else: Do you think you will ever regret taking up your cross and following Christ? I believe the only regret you may have is that you did not always go where he led you and did not always give what he asked of you. Ultimately, the way of the cross is the way of no regrets. It is the way that makes our lives fruitful and gives our lives eternal worth.

Years ago, I was given a book titled *Memorial Stones: Spiritual Epics in the Life of George and Annie Matthews*. George Matthews served as a pastor in the Methodist Church and his wife, Annie, was a leader in the Women's Missionary Society of their Methodist conference. George and Annie lived with Annie's parents, both of whom were deeply involved in the church. In fact, Annie's father was the Methodist district superintendent.

Eventually, God brought George to surrender his life to Christ so totally that he was transformed as a Christian and a pastor. He found himself burdened to share with his people the depths and richness of a truly surrendered life, so he invited a certain Holiness evangelist to come and hold revival services in his church. George's wife was not happy about this. Neither was her father, the district superintendent, so Annie Matthews argued with George about what his decision would do to their reputations. If this evangelist came, George's standing in the conference would be damaged and her role in the missionary society would come to an end.

When Annie saw that her husband intended to go ahead, she had an honest conversation with God. To her surprise, God began to reveal things in her heart that were not pleasing to him. She became aware that she had never surrendered certain things to God. "I found that there was a fear of men inside me greater than the desire to please God," she said. "I wanted the approval of my peers and my friends, and I wanted my husband to have the approval of his peers."

Annie Matthews began to pray with more earnestness. Slowly, God forced the issue. "Do you want their approval or mine?" was his question to her. Annie was finally able to say, "O God, I want your approval—even if it drives a wedge between me and my parents, even if it ruins my reputation in the women's work."

The Holy Spirit filled Annie's soul and broke the power of that desire to protect herself and her reputation. He set her free to live in love for Christ and others. In fact, my own salvation was a fruit of her obedience. The salvation of my family came as a result of Annie Matthews's decision to go the way of the cross.

God would penetrate and sanctify every relationship that you have, whether with people or things. He would place the cross between you and everything else so that you see all of life in its shadow. Annie Matthews loved Jesus enough to embrace his cross. Her prayer became, "Jesus first."

## THE PRAYER OF A SURRENDERED HEART

Do you run from the sacrifice that is required by the cross? Until your heart is spiritually cleansed, the cross will strike fear within you. Surrender to God enables you to bear the cross humbly and even with joy for Christ's sake because you know it is God's will for you. Have you ever shared the reproach of Christ? Has it ever cost you anything to be faithful to him? That's what I mean by bearing the cross with Jesus.

It was not easy for David Livingstone to leave England and go to Africa with the message of Christ. It was not easy for his wife to follow him there. It was not easy for Robert Morrison to go to China and spend most of his life there before he saw a single convert.

And what about Allen Gardiner, an early missionary to the Patagonian islands? His supply ship was delayed and Gardiner starved to death. Two weeks after he died, the ship arrived and the crew found his body sitting where he had been writing. Do you know the last words he penned in his journal? "Great and marvelous are the loving kindnesses of my gracious Lord with me." This man had prayed that he might win the Patagonians to Christ regardless of the cost, and the triune God took his prayer seriously. What Gardiner wasn't able to do in his life, God did through his death, because all of England was challenged by his example. The work of God was advanced more by his death than it could have been had he lived.

This is the way of the cross. Nothing is ever lost if we go that way.

I am convinced that bearing Christ's burdens in prayer is the only way we can redemptively overcome evil in this world, because evil cannot be conquered by brute force. Forced obedience to God is the way of hell, not heaven.

Certainly, God will conquer all evil forces on the Last Day; however, that will not be a redemptive conquest. God's word on that day will be, "Let him who does wrong continue to do wrong; let him who is vile continue to be vile; let him who does right continue to do right; and let him who is holy continue to be holy" (Rev 22:11).

No, the redemption of evil came on Good Friday, when God the Father stood aside and let his Son suffer. That day, he allowed the Enemy to wield his power, but the Enemy's apparent victory over Christ was evil's undoing. When God allowed evil to be imposed upon his Son, who took the world's evil into himself, the world was saved from evil. Likewise, in prayer we can take into our hearts the brokenness, sin, and need of other people; we can let the sin of the world meet the Spirit of Christ living in us. Then our prayer becomes redemptive, like the cross.

David Brainerd and Henry Martyn were two of the greatest missionary examples of bearing the cross of Christ around the world. Brainerd died as a young man, trying to evangelize the Indians of

New England. When his journal was published in England, it inspired Henry Martyn, a brilliant student at Cambridge, to leave his studies and become a missionary to India. However, Martyn fell ill and died before he reached the mission field. Church historian Leonard W. Bacon wrote, "To what purpose was this waste? Out of that early grave of Brainerd and that lonely grave of Martyn far away by the splashing of the Euxine [Black] Sea, has sprung the noble army of modern missionaries."[1] They accomplished through suffering and death all that they dreamed to do in life.

## PAUL'S PRAYERS IN SUFFERING

The apostle Paul was put in prison in Philippi and given a severe flogging, but the jailer's entire family was saved and one of the most important churches of the first century was established. In later years, Paul was imprisoned in Rome when he wrote his letter to the Philippians and the imperial palace guard heard the gospel of Christ. How could Paul complain about his circumstances if they furthered the knowledge of the gospel? He embraced his suffering, confident that it would allow God to work his redemptive purposes.

Consider briefly the tenets of Paul's sacrificial faith. First, he was absolutely sure that the God he met on the Damascus road was in charge of human history. He believed that evil and suffering will not have the final word, but God will. So Paul wrote with confidence that a day was drawing near when every knee would bow to Christ and things would turn right side up.

Second, Paul believed God was seeking a family—children for the Father and a Bride for his Son. Worldly kingdoms can be built on power, but families cannot. Families can only be built on love. The condition for love is freedom, with all of its attendant possibilities. When one bears a child or chooses a mate, that child may choose to be a prodigal or a loving child and that spouse may decide to be

---

1. As quoted in Duane V. Maxey, *2700-Plus Sermon Illustrations* (Chandler, AZ: Holiness Data Ministry, 2001), no. 2544.

faithful or not. The heartaches of our world result from our misuse of the freedoms God has given us. This is a paradox. However, the God we worship is a God of both power and love. A relationship created by God's imposition of brute power would be quite different from the loving relationship that comes as a result of our free choice. Yes, God is omnipotent, and his omnipotence is clearly manifested in his creation. Yet love is the essence of his nature, so it characterizes his relationship with his family. Power does not characterize the relationship of the three persons of the Trinity. Their relationship is one of love, and into that relationship God has invited us. Power will ultimately characterize God's relationship to those who reject him and his will, and he will reign over them in his omnipotence. But the eternal relationship of the Father with his children and of God's Son with his Bride is one of love. This is why W. H. Auden said:

> If, as Christians believe, God is love, then, in one sense he is not omnipotent, for he cannot compel his creatures to accept his love without ceasing to be himself. The wrath of God is not his wrath but the way in which those feel his love who refuse it, and the right of refusal is a privilege which not even their Creator can take from them.[2]

Third, Paul believed that God's love holds the ultimate answer to the problems produced by our human freedom. He believed that God's love will eventually prevail because the Lover enters into and shares the suffering of those he seeks. He chooses to bear the consequences of his loved ones' unbelief and disobedience. So God took into himself all of the suffering, sin, and death that we human beings initiated by our actions. God knew when he created Adam that he himself would pay the highest price to regain his family; but because of his love for us he committed to pay that price in the person of his Son dying on the cross.

---

2. As quoted in Charles Williams, *The Descent of the Dove* (New York: Oxford University Press, 1939), viii.

Fourth, Paul believed that no pain suffered in love is meaningless. In a world without sin, suffering would have been a contradiction; but in a fallen world, the absence of suffering would have been a lie. Paul believed that pain is the very hope of a world that has betrayed God: not the pain that we endure as a consequence of our disobedience, but the pain that our divine Lover experienced when he assumed the consequences of our own misuse of freedom. The pain we have brought upon ourselves can be relieved only by being assumed by another who did not deserve it. That is the truth of the cross.

Charles Williams in his own idiosyncratic way says that a principle of exchange runs through all of existence and even characterizes the interpersonal life of the triune Godhead. He writes, "Nobody can carry his own burdens; he only can, and therefore he must, carry someone else's."[3] His wording may seem a bit strange, but it helps us make sense out of these other words from the writer of the epistle to the Hebrews:

> Let us fix our eyes on Jesus, the author and perfecter of our faith, who for the joy set before him, endured the cross, scorning its shame, and sat down at the right hand of the throne of God. Consider him who endured such opposition from sinful men, so that you will not grow weary and lose heart. (Heb 12:2–3)

Finally, Paul makes it clear that God the Father, who made Jesus' sufferings beneficial, will also make ours beneficial when we identify with the sin and suffering of the world as Christ did. This truth has become very meaningful to me. It has made a difference in how I view suffering when I encounter it in my own life or the lives of people I love. Christ's example teaches us that the crosses we bear and the suffering we endure can become tools to accomplish the eternal purposes of God.

A woman in labor knows that life does not come easily in the physical world. The same is true in the spiritual world. In fact,

---

3. Ibid., vi.

intercessory prayer may be called the travail of the Spirit of God in a human heart as it yearns to see the birth of another human soul. I can think of no better analogy of intercessory prayer than that of an expectant mother in labor pains.

We need to ask, "God, what spiritual burden do you have for me to bear?" When that becomes clear, our only proper response is to embrace that burden and bear it until the hour of delivery has come. It will be worth the wait.

The last time my wife was pregnant, I was walking down the hospital hallway when the doctor saw me and said, "I hope you have plenty of bedroom space in your house."

"What do you mean?" I asked.

"You have two little girls in there!"

"You're lying," I exclaimed. We had three children already, and I was in graduate school. Elsie and I did not own a home, and I did not have a job.

Bemused, the doctor said, "Go and see."

In those days, fathers were not normally allowed in the delivery room, but I walked in and looked down into the bassinet. There lay two little girls wiggling against each other like two bloody earthworms. I stared at them in disbelief. Elsie asked, "How many?"

"Two."

"Are you sure?"

"Very sure."

"Are they all right?" she asked quietly.

"They look all right to me."

"How many did you say?"

I raised fingers over her face and repeated, "Two."

In a burst of joy, Elsie said, "Isn't that just like the Lord? You ask for one and you get two!" All the burden of the previous nine months was forgotten when we saw those tiny babies.

Perhaps you are in the middle of a spiritual pregnancy. Perhaps you are weary of bearing the burden of prayer that Christ has placed on your heart. It truly is burdensome, but don't walk away from it.

Pastor, don't look for another church.

Missionary, don't walk away from your colleagues.

Parent, don't give up on your children.

Husband/wife, don't disengage from your family or desert your spouse.

Just remember that God's timing is never the same as ours, and any effort to give birth prematurely can create many problems. You want to see a delivery of your burden in the fullness of God's time. Only then will the glory come. For all those crosses you bear in prayer, you can be sure that God has a resurrection day.

# 7

## WHEN GOD MEETS
## THE WORLD IN A HUMAN HEART

### ALL THERE IS OF US, FOR ALL THERE IS OF HIM
### FOR ALL THAT HE WANTS TO DO THROUGH US
### TO REACH A LOST WORLD.

—VISION STATEMENT OF THE ORIENTAL MISSIONARY SOCIETY, 1901

 A desire for meaning burns within every person. We want our lives to count. However, there are times when nearly everyone says, "What can I do that would be significant? How can I make a difference in this world?" Additionally, a Christian asks, "How can I do anything redemptive amid the enormous conflicts and problems I see everywhere?"

The Scriptures insist that one person indeed can make a difference. The Old Testament often shows God searching for an intercessor; again and again, God declares that if he can find one person to intercede, the destruction of many people can be averted. Here are some examples:

> This is what the LORD says:
> "Where is your mother's certificate of divorce with which I
>     sent her away?
> Or to which of my creditors did I sell you?
> Because of your sins you were sold;
>     because of your transgressions your mother was sent away.

"When I came, why was there no one?
    When I called, why was there no one to answer?
Was my arm too short to ransom you?
    Do I lack the strength to rescue you?
By a mere rebuke I dry up the sea, I turn rivers into a desert;
    their fish rot for lack of water and die of thirst." (Isa 50:1–2)


Truth is nowhere to be found and whoever shuns evil becomes
    a prey.
The LORD looked and was displeased that there was no justice.
He saw that there was no one,
    he was appalled that there was no one to intervene;
so his own arm worked salvation for him,
    and his own righteousness sustained him. (Isa 59:15–16)


For the day of vengeance was in my heart,
    and the year of my redemption has come.
I looked, but there was no one to help,
    I was appalled that no one gave support;
so my own arm worked salvation for me,
    and my own wrath sustained me. (Isa 63:4–5)


Go up and down the streets of Jerusalem, look around and
    consider,
    search through her squares.
If you can find but *one person* who deals honestly and seeks
    the truth,
    I will forgive this city. (Jer 5:1, emphasis added)


I looked for *a man* among them who would build up the wall
    and stand before me in the gap on behalf of the land
so I would not have to destroy it, but I found none.
    (Ezek 22:30, emphasis added)

These passages show us two amazing things. First, they indicate that the omnipotent God who controls everything must work within the limitations of the world that he created. We think the problem with our humanity is that we are not in total control of our circumstances. Yet God, the omnipotent One, has circumstances of his own creation. In these texts, he is saying, "If I could find the right person, my circumstances would be altered. I would not have to do what my justice demands that I do."

Second, we find that God is often unable to find such a person to help him. This intrigues us because God knows all things, yet Omniscience is surprised and Omnipotence seeks our help. It seems strange to us, but this is what the biblical texts say.

## The Importance of an Intercessor

Let us focus especially on the passage from Jeremiah 5, which says that God looked for one person to intercede on behalf of the city of Jerusalem. Jerusalem was the "Holy City" itself—the chosen city, the city of God, where the temple of God stood and where he resided. The Jews called Jerusalem "the navel of the earth" because that was where the blessings of God's grace were to come down and spread across the world. Yet Jerusalem became as debauched and corrupted as the worst heathen metropolis. So God said, "If I can find just one person who lives right, loves the truth, and does justly, I can forgive the 'Holy City' of all its sin."

Likewise, the other four passages say that one temporal person can make a difference to the eternal God. One contingent person can make a difference to the sovereign God. When I began working with these five passages, the one that intrigued me most was Isaiah 59. It begins with God saying, "My arm is not short that it cannot save and my ear is not heavy that it cannot hear." In other words, God says, "There is nothing lacking in my power," because his arm is a symbol of personal power. He says, "There's nothing lacking in my compassion," for his ear symbolizes his attentiveness to his people's need. So there's nothing wrong with God's power or his heart; he is able and eager to save everyone. After all, he is the-God-Who-Saves. So what's the problem? Why is the world in such a mess?

Isaiah 59 is an Old Testament parallel to Romans 1, which describes the results of human depravity. Isaiah 59 paints a dismal picture of the moral and spiritual state of the Jewish nation. The full force of its condemnation is directed at the city of God, which is the center of the problem. The well-being of the world hangs on the people of God—and they have failed their duty.

I believe this is a neglected aspect of the biblical doctrine of election. God's saving work is always done mediatorially, so he called Israel to become the people through whom he could accomplish his divine purpose in the world. God's own people became the key to the world's salvation. We tend to wonder why any ethnic group would be privileged to bear the title of "God's Chosen People," yet they were not chosen for a life of privilege. They were chosen to live redemptively among the other peoples God had created—and they failed him.

The same is true of the church. When the church decries the tragic lostness of the world, the source of the problem is likely to be the church itself.

This underscores the importance of revival among the people of God. Revival begins everything good in the world, and it must start within the assembly of believers. The repentance needed within a society can begin only when God's own people repent. That is why the great prophets of the Old Testament were sent to Jerusalem instead of Egypt, Assyria, or Babylon. They knew that if God's people were spiritually clean, the world had a chance. Unfortunately, this is the opposite of the way most of us tend to think about changing the world.

In Isaiah 59, God says to his people, "You have separated yourselves from me by your sin and darkness. Justice has fallen in the streets of the holy city. The moral darkness is so deep that one needs to light lamps at noon" (see vv 1–9). So God looks for one person to intercede for him. He seeks one person through whom he can speak and work.

What does God mean when he asks for an "intercessor"? The Hebrew word translated as "intercessor" (Isa 59:16 KJV) is *maphgia'*, derived from the Hebrew word *paga'*, which means "to meet." In fact, *mapghi'* is the causative participle of the verb "to meet," so a *mapghia'* is "one who causes to meet." Isaiah is literally saying that God needs someone who will bring him and his world together, someone who will become the conduit for his grace.

I wondered how often that causative form of this verb appeared in the Old Testament. When I checked my Hebrew lexicon, I found only six occurrences. Three of them are in Isaiah, so they are useful keys to help us understand what is meant in Isaiah 59. The first of the other two occurrences is Isaiah 53:12:

> Therefore I will give him a portion among the great,
> and he will divide the spoils with the strong,
> because he poured out his life unto death,
> and was numbered with the transgressors.
> For he bore the sin of many,
> and made intercession for the transgressors.

This closing verse of the chapter gives us Isaiah's picture of God's suffering servant, a prophecy that found its fulfillment in the incarnation and passion of Christ. He poured out his life to death, was numbered because of this with the transgressors, took upon himself the sin of the transgressors, and thus made intercession for them. So Jesus was a *maphgia'*. The other passage is verse 6 of the same chapter, a verse familiar to most of us:

> We all, like sheep, have gone astray, each of us has turned to his own way; and the LORD has laid on him the iniquity of us all.

The phrase is usually translated, "and the Lord laid on him the iniquity of us all," but it can be read quite differently. The verb translated as "laid" is again the causative form of *paga'*, so it could be translated, "caused to meet." The Hebrew preposition translated "on" is more often translated as "in" (as in the opening verse of the Bible, "*In* the beginning . . ." [Gen 1:1]). This verse now gives us a significant insight into the power of Calvary. What did Christ come to do there? He came to be our *maphgia'*—the intercessor in whom the adequacy of God could meet the sinful needs of our hearts. Christ provided a way for God's salvation to meet the world's brokenness by taking that brokenness *into* himself. My preference would be to translate verse 6 as

> We all, like sheep, have gone astray, each of us has turned to to his own way; and Yahweh has caused to meet *in him* the iniquity of us all.

I like rendering the Hebrew preposition with "into" rather than "on," because the passage indicates a much closer identification with our burden than the word *on* would imply. The statement that our iniquity was laid "on" him suggests that he was assigned the legal penalty for our offenses. There is more here though. He did more than take the consequences of our sins on himself; he took the *problem* that produced those consequences. He assumed our sin itself. As Paul says in 2 Corinthians 5:21, "God made him who had no sin to be sin for us, so that in him we might become the righteousness of God." Without ever sinning, Christ became sin itself. He took our evil into himself so that our world could be delivered from evil. The world's evil became his evil, though he never committed a bit of it. And by assuming our evil, he defeated the death that resulted from it.

The early church fathers had an expression for this truth: "unassumed, unhealed." In other words, if Christ did not assume our sin, he did not heal it. But he did assume our sin. He made it his own and provided deliverance from all of its uncleanness and bondage, as well as its penalty. *In* him our redemption took place.

After reading that, I went back to Isaiah 59:15–16, where I found this interesting example of that verb:

> The Lord looked and was displeased
>> that there was no justice.
> He saw that there was no one,
>> he was appalled that there was *no one to intervene*;
> so his own arm worked salvation for him
>> and his own righteousness sustained him. (emphasis added)

Admittedly, it is difficult for us to grasp biblical ways of thinking because they are so different from our modern ways. However, this text says that when God could not find a human intercessor, his own right arm brought salvation to his people. He used his "arm" (his personal power) to solve the problem.

Significantly, there are eleven references to the "arm of the Lord" in chapters 40–66 of Isaiah. The prophet foresees a day when God cannot find help from anyone, so his own "arm" will have to do the job. Perhaps we should think more seriously about the implications of God's having to use his own "arm."

When I was in graduate school, I read a lot of ancient mythology: Egyptian, Babylonian, Greek, Roman, and Hittite. A recurring figure of Greek mythology is that of Zeus, the head of the Greek pantheon, standing atop Mount Olympus, the mountain of the gods. He raises his right arm, lifting high a lightning bolt. The point is clear: If Zeus sees anything down below that he does not like, he will throw his lightning bolt of destruction and strike the people who displease him! He will correct any problem on earth with his powerful arm. The arm of Zeus was ready to solve any human problem. So when we wonder, "Why doesn't God strike down the transgressors?" we are quite pagan in our thinking.

Isaiah 53:1 says, "Who has believed our message? And to whom has the arm of the Lord been revealed?" In other words, Isaiah's understanding of God's power is not at all like ours. Zeus with his lightning bolt fits our thinking. Yet this is not the kind of Person that God is. Rather, he hangs on a cross on a desolate rock while his creatures impose their power upon him. Instead of pouring his wrath on us in Zeus fashion, he allows us to pour our wrath on him. Isaiah 53 is a picture of the arm of the Lord; it is a picture of Jesus. We pour our wrath on him and *into* him. When he has absorbed all of sin and death that we can impose on him, he overcomes it.

This is what the prophet means when he says the Lord Jesus was wounded for our transgressions and bruised for our iniquities. We did not revere Jesus Christ as God, but considered him to be stricken, smitten of God, and afflicted. Even so, the power of God was at work in him, accepting into his pure heart all of the evil of human history. Evil did not destroy him, although it did kill him. When he opened himself to receive the world's evil, he bore us in his heart.

God says, "When I could not find one, my own arm brought salvation." When God could not find an intercessor, he became one. So Isaiah 59:16 is a promise of God's own incarnation.

God could not solve the sin problem by remaining in heaven, because the problem was not there. Nor could he solve it in himself, because it was not in him. The problem had to be solved where it was—in the human heart. That is why Bethlehem was necessary. The only remedy for our sin was for God to become one of us. So the eternal Son left the freedom of heaven for the constriction of Mary's womb; he laid aside the glory of heaven for the humbleness of a human life. Through the power of the Spirit of God, who was the source of his conception and the motive of his unusual life, Jesus solved the problem of sin in one human being, himself. Then the cross made that solution available for the entire human race.

## Burden Bearing: The Attitude of Intercession

Our salvation depended on Christ's decision to make our problem his. Therefore, it is no accident that the major Old Testament word for "forgive" is the Hebrew *nasa'*, which means simply "to bear."

The only Man without sin solved the problem of our sin by bearing it within himself. He reached the point where someone else's well-being was more important than his own. That is the essential mission of an intercessor, and it is the essential nature of God's love.

In pastors' conferences and seminary classes, I find few people who believe this. Someone seeking a pastorate will ask about the salary, the parsonage, the health benefits, the number of people in attendance, the opportunities for professional advancement, and so on. A pastoral candidate asks these questions because he is thinking about his position and status instead of the people who need him, so his ministry is blighted before it starts. Ministry can be fruitful only when you get so close to the heart of God that he can say to you, "Look over there. I care about those people. I would like to see them reached with the gospel, but that will happen only if someone cares about them as I do. And I care more about them than I do about myself."

A successful businessman told me, "I would like to die penniless. I don't want to be responsible for leaving assets when I go to be with the Lord. I want it all to be in his service." It has been interesting to watch his impact around the world as he makes himself and his resources available to God. He knows that others are more important to him than he is. Christ has put his own heart into this man's heart, so this man is willing to bear the world in his soul. He is free to pour himself out for anything God lays on his heart.

I was in my sixties before I realized the full impact of 2 Corinthians 5:15. I was familiar with verse 14, which says, "For Christ's love compels us, because we are convinced that one died for all, and therefore all died." But then verse 15 says, "And he died for all, that those who live *should no longer live for themselves* but for him who died for them and was raised again" (emphasis added). Christ died to make me a *maphgia'*, an intercessor who would bear the burdens of the world as he did.

How can our troubled world be changed? Only by God's people being scattered through all levels of society and allowing God to put his burdens in our hearts. Then we will see a city changed because a humble person has been praying, "I will not let you go, Lord, until you move in this place." Then we will see the Spirit of God change the small, insignificant, unseen places of our world. Communications media may not pay any attention to these "navels of the world," but God knows every one of them. He is looking for people who will pour out their lives for others in his name.

The sin of the world must become our personal problem. We must step into the world and its needs. The Holy Spirit can enable us to carry the world in our hearts so that its lostness is our burden and all of our personal burdens are given to Christ. I believe God has a portion of his world for every Christian to bear in prayer.

I have an Australian friend who worked for several years as a newspaper reporter and was a bit of an atheist. In her work, she met some Christian leaders who wanted newspaper publicity for the work they were doing. One was quite arrogant and offensive. An argument resulted. This Christian leader threatened to take her to the ethics commission of the Australian Journalists Association. She assured him she would be happy to go.

The next day, as she was sitting at her desk, in walked one of the Christian men who had been with the preacher who had so offended her the day before. He was a local pastor, and he was carrying a dozen roses. "I want to apologize for my friend yesterday," he said. "I'm so sorry."

Amused, she took his bouquet of flowers.

Six months later, she was assigned to write a series of articles on the drug rehabilitation programs of Brisbane, Australia. As part of her research, she visited a Christian center for drug addicts and discovered that it was operated by the same pastor who had given her flowers. His presence startled her, but she would not be deterred from her assignment. She stayed to observe the rehab program for six days. As she was conducting her final interview with the pastor, she suddenly found herself weeping. "I don't know what you have here," she said, "but I would give anything in the world to have it too."

"You *can* have it," he said.

"How?" she asked. "I'm an atheist. You said this is all wrapped up in your religion."

"Inextricably," he smiled, "but that is no problem. Just tell Jesus about it."

That is how she found Jesus. Only then did she learn that the Christians in Brisbane had been praying for her those six months. One Australian pastor was willing to love an atheist, despite the hostility and rejection he initially experienced from her. Because of that love, she found the joy of knowing Christ.

As believers, we have the privilege of introducing hostile unbelievers to the love of Jesus. Their lives can be transformed only when they encounter *his* life in *our* lives.

# 8

## BEARING THE WORLD AS JESUS DID

JESUS WANTS US TO LIVE FOR
OTHER PEOPLE AS HE LIVED;
HE WANTS US TO LOVE OTHER PEOPLE
AS HE LOVED US.

Prayer will always have an element of mystery because it involves a personal relationship, and relationships have some aspects that we cannot comprehend. No matter how intimately we know another person, we are aware of depths that we have not probed and perhaps never can. In fact, there are depths in ourselves that we are not sure we know. Moreover, in prayer we are not face to face with another finite creature but with the eternal source of all being, God himself. He is the One on whom we are totally dependent and by whose graciousness we draw every breath. Paul often calls our relationship with God a great mystery (Eph 5:32; Col 1:27; 1 Tim 3:16), so it is little wonder that prayer leaves us with some baffling questions.

The most mysterious aspect of prayer is one that we seldom notice: Scripture tells us that God himself prays. That usually comes as a bit of a shock. It did for me.

I recall discussing this with a pastor friend of mine. "Why do you think we need to pray?" I asked. "Doesn't God know all things?

Am I telling God something he does not know?" My friend assured me that God knows all things, but he wants to hear our requests.

"So why does God pray?" I persisted.

My friend laughed. "Kinlaw, God doesn't pray!" So I asked him to explain these passages in Romans 8 and Hebrews 7:

> In the same way, the Spirit helps us in our weakness. We do not know what we ought to pray for, but *the Spirit himself intercedes for us* with groans that words cannot express. And he who searches our hearts knows the mind of the Spirit, because *the Spirit intercedes for the saints* in accordance with God's will. (Rom 8:26–27, emphasis added)

> If God is for us, who can be against us? He who did not spare his own Son, but gave him up for us all—how will he not also, along with him, graciously give us all things? Who will bring any charge against those whom God has chosen? Who is he that condemns? Christ Jesus who died—more than that, who was raised to life—*is at the right hand of God and is also interceding for us.* (Rom 8:31–34, emphasis added)

> Therefore he is able to save completely those who come to God through him, because *he always lives to intercede for them.* (Heb 7:25, emphasis added)

My friend was stumped, just as I was. However, these passages make clear that prayer is infinitely more than asking a benevolent God to meet the needs and desires of the person who's praying. Prayer is more than asking and receiving. Obviously, it is a bigger business than I thought if the second and third persons of the triune Godhead devote themselves continually to it!

The mediatorial principle is operating here. The Son and the Spirit are not praying for themselves, but for us. This explains why Jesus insisted that his disciples should pray in his name. We do not come to the Father on our own; we come with and through Jesus.

All things come to us *from* the Father, *through* the Son, *by* the Holy Spirit. Our relationship with the Father is never immediate; it is mediated through the Son. So Jesus said, "I am the way and the truth and the life. No one comes to the Father except through me" (John 14:6). We deal with God through the Son. We know this is true in the matter of salvation, but it is also true in the matter of prayer.

Old Testament Hebrew has a rich variety of words for prayer. Since prayer is a conversation between persons, it is not surprising to find that the simple Hebrew word for "speak" or "say" is often used. There is also a word for "call upon" or "ask"; two words for "cry out"; one for "entreat the favor of"; and another word for "petition" or "supplicate." The Hebrew verb most commonly translated as "pray" is *hithpallel,* which means "to interpose oneself," and the normal word for "prayer" in the Old Testament is the noun form of that verb, *tephillah.* So at the heart of the Old Testament concept of prayer is the mediatorial idea of standing between two persons or interposing oneself to facilitate dialogue between them. This suggests that we are praying best, and most authentically doing what prayer is about, when we are praying for someone else.

It also helps us to understand that Jesus is continuing to do for us now in heaven what he did here on earth. His work of atonement was completed in the cross and the resurrection, but his role as mediator began before the creation and continues until the end of time. He and the Father gave us life, so they continue to carry us in their hearts. There is a reflection of this in human relations, for parents never stop caring for their children. No matter how old they are, our children are always a part of us, and we are always a part of them—whether or not they want us to be.

Jesus graphically described his mediatorial ministry when he was here in the flesh. For example,

> I am the good shepherd. The good shepherd lays down his life for the sheep. The hired hand is not the shepherd who owns the sheep. So when he sees the wolf coming, he abandons the sheep

and runs away. Then the wolf attacks the flock and scatters it. (John 10:11–12)

Notice that the welfare of the sheep is dependent upon the shepherd, upon his compassion and kindness, even his willingness to sacrifice himself for the sheep. That is where Christ drew a distinction between a good shepherd and a hired hand. The good shepherd puts the welfare of the sheep ahead of his own. He cares more for them than he cares for himself, while the hireling cares ultimately for himself. Note what Jesus says further:

I am the good shepherd; I know my sheep and my sheep know me, just as the Father knows me and I know the Father—I lay down my life for the sheep. I have other sheep that are not of this sheep pen. I must bring them also. They too will listen to my voice, and there shall be one flock and one shepherd. The reason my Father loves me is that I lay down my life—only to take it up again. No one takes it from me, but I lay it down of my own accord. I have authority to lay it down and authority to take it up again. This command I received from my Father. (John 10:14–18)

The major difference between Jesus and other religious leaders was the other-centeredness of Jesus and the self-centeredness of others. There lay the secret of Christ's power. It is why he condemned the self-centeredness of hireling religious leaders.

Jesus commanded his disciples to follow his example, loving others as he loves them. He called them to be good shepherds as well:

My command is this: Love each other as I have loved you. Greater love has no one than this, that he lay down his life for his friends. You are my friends if you do what I command. I no longer call you servants, because a servant does not know his master's business. Instead, I have called you friends, for everything that I learned from my Father I have made known to you. (John 15:12–15)

What made Jesus' love redemptive was not his power to perform miracles; he could redeem them from the consequences of sin only by sacrificing himself on the cross. And he calls us to live that way.

The apostle Paul tells us that other-centered, self-sacrificing love is the nature of the Father as well as of the Son. He says that if we are to please God, we must act like the Father and the Son. Note Paul's counsel to the Ephesians:

Therefore be imitators of God, as beloved children, and live in love, as Christ loved us and gave himself up for us, a fragrant offering and sacrifice to God. (Eph 5:1–2 NRSV)

Jesus wants us to live for other people as he lived; he wants to put in our hearts his own love for others, which is greater than his love for himself. He opens his soul to us, and it is a soul of agape love—love not for the sake of what others can do for him but for what he can do for them.

Intercession involves interposing ourselves between God himself and a person in need. The most important result of intercession is not a change in the circumstances of a person for whom we are praying but a change in the person's heart. That is not easy! Even God has difficulty changing people's hearts.

God gave human beings certain freedoms, and he allows those freedoms to put conditions on his sovereign power. In other words, he made us enough like him that we are capable of creating problems for him.

God will not force us to love him, because he seeks love that is freely given. So conditions must be right for even God to transform us. You see, God is dealing with people and not things; if he were dealing with things, God would simply do as he wishes.

When God's people were without water in the wilderness, God told Moses, "Strike the rock" (Ex 17:6 NRSV) and water came gushing out. God had no difficulty making the rock accomplish his purposes; but he had an exceedingly difficult time changing the rocky hearts of Moses and his people.

In the New Testament, Jesus said, "If anyone is thirsty, let him come to me and drink. Whoever believes in me, as the Scripture has said, streams of living water will flow within him" (John 7:37–38). God had no problem providing physical water; but for spiritual water to flow, a person must thirst for it and drink of it. The Spirit can give someone that spiritual thirst, but only the individual can decide to drink and believe.

Jesus had no problem healing physical blindness. Mark 8 tells about a blind man Jesus touched, who then saw men as trees walking around. Jesus touched him again and he saw clearly. Mark 10 is about blind Bartimaeus; Jesus touched his eyes once and he saw perfectly. Between these two stories about physical blindness, Mark describes the spiritual blindness of the Twelve when Jesus foretold his death on the cross. They could not understand what he came to do. Jesus had no problem curing people's physical blindness, but he had an exceedingly difficult time with the spiritual blindness of his own disciples.

# 9

## "My Grace Is Sufficient for You"

### We are simply the means through which God can work. Failure to understand this can be tragic.

God wants to work through you and me to reach others. This can occur through our preaching, witnessing, and serving, but preeminently through our praying. When we pray for God to influence the lives of others, God puts his burden for them within us and moves us to help him reach them.

In all of this, there is one danger: We may get a false notion of what our role is. We can easily forget that there is nothing redemptive in what we do in God's service; we are simply the means through which God can do his saving work. Failure to understand this can be tragic.

The story of Moses graphically illustrates the point. Numbers 20 describes a decisive event toward the close of the Hebrews' journey to Canaan when Moses faced a problem that had occurred before: There was no water and the people began complaining bitterly. They turned against Moses and Aaron, who consequently turned to God for help. God told them to gather all of Israel before a great rock. Then Moses was to speak to the rock in the name of Yahweh to give them water and water would gush from it to satisfy the thirsty Hebrews.

In his anger, however, Moses asked the multitude, "Listen, you rebels, must *we* bring you water out of this rock?" (v 10, emphasis added). He then raised his staff and struck the rock twice. Water gushed out of it and the people were satisfied. But God was not. After all, God told Moses to speak to the rock, not strike it.

When a similar situation occurred earlier in their journey, God had told Moses to strike a rock and water would come from it (Ex 17:6). This time he told his servant to speak to the rock, not strike it. In Moses' irritation, he made a tragic mistake, so God denied him and Aaron the privilege of entering the Promised Land (Num 20:12).

For years, I thought God was unusually harsh on Moses here. Moses may well have been one of the greatest men who ever lived, other than Jesus himself. Think of all that he endured to lead Israel from Egypt to Canaan! Could not God overlook one slip-up? But as the years have passed and I have come to understand more fully the mediatorial principle of God's work, I have come to realize why God did this. Nothing is more crucial to God's work than for us to know with crystal clarity the difference between what we can do and what God can do. If we trust our own ability, there will be tragic consequences. Humility is indispensable in a Christian worker. We must realize that we are totally dependent upon God and his Spirit. God will not share his glory with us, because that would be a lie, so our actions must always point beyond ourselves to him.

Paul implied this when he spoke of Christ in us as the "hope of glory" (Col 1:27; see also Rom 5:2). We never will be anyone's hope of glory; that hope comes from Christ alone, even though we can be the means through which Christ can reach needy souls. We can be the means, but only if we are very clear that Christ is who the people need, not us. There must be no confusion of roles here.

The last four chapters of 2 Corinthians are particularly telling in this respect. Paul is deeply concerned about the spiritual welfare of the church at Corinth because some false teachers are misleading the Corinthian believers. Paul condemns these leaders for offering the people another gospel, another Christ, and another spirit. Paul challenges their credentials. To do this, he must speak of his own. Clearly he is very uncomfortable about this task, but too much is at stake for him to remain silent.

So here Paul gives us more autobiographical material than we find in any of his other letters. He speaks of his suffering for Christ as he was stoned, beaten, shipwrecked, and imprisoned (2 Cor 11:16–33). The false teachers claim their superior spirituality is proven by their visions and ecstatic experiences. So Paul responds with an account of his own vision of being taken up into the third heaven, where he experienced things too sacred to be described, even if Paul had language adequate to the occasion.

Yet the theme of Paul's *inadequacy* runs throughout this account. He does not talk about his strengths, but rather his weaknesses. Thirteen times in these four chapters, he uses some form of the Greek word our Bible translations render as "weakness." He does not draw attention to his greatness—just the opposite. He reminds the Corinthians of his inadequacy.

In fact, Paul tells us a fascinating story of how God impressed this fact upon him with a "thorn in my flesh" (2 Cor 12:7). He says God gave him this persistent problem, "a messenger of Satan," to torment him. Paul felt this was a hindrance to his ministry, so he urged God three times to remove it, but the Lord would not. Instead, God reminded Paul of his own divine grace. He said, "My grace is sufficient for you, for my power is made perfect in weakness" (v 9). Paul responded by saying, "I will boast all the more gladly about my weaknesses, so that Christ's power may rest on me" (v 9).

We can so easily become presumptuous in this regard. This is why God gave the apostle a weakness that made him perpetually conscious of his dependence on God for the grace to serve in Christ's name. In fact, Paul's statement is stronger than our English translations suggest. The Greek word translated as "weakness" literally means "strengthlessness"; *astheneia* is built on the word *sthenos* ("strength") with the Greek privative *a-* ("no" or "not"). So Paul confesses his "strengthlessness," not just his "weakness." He is not saying that he needs God to increase his strength, but rather that he needs divine power to accomplish the work at all. This is what Paul means by God's "grace" (v 9).

It is not difficult to connect Paul's experience with that of Moses and the rock. We can imagine God telling Paul something like this: "Paul, do not bring this up again. My grace is sufficient for your weakness. My power is perfected in your strengthlessness. I want my power to be seen in you, so stay strengthless. Then it will be clear that what happens in your ministry is not your work but mine. There must be no confusion here. If you live out of your strengthlessness, then I can do great things through you. If you understand this is my work and not yours, then we can proceed. But you must know that we are not building the kingdom together, Paul—it is I alone. You are simply the occasion for my working, so don't confuse an occasion with a cause. Let's keep this clear."

Paul got the message. He said that he did not boast in his gifts but in the power of God working through him. As a result, he could delight in opposition, in insults, in hardships, in persecutions, in difficulties of every kind. These were no longer his problems but God's. God had denied Paul's prayer at one level but answered it on another. God knew that Paul's deepest desire was to be divinely used, so the apostle had no desire to share God's glory.

As I meditated on this, I remembered a conversation with a friend who was associated with the San Diego Opera Company. He had a magnificent voice, and I loved to hear him sing. One day I said, "I have a question. From what I understand, operatic singers—even the best ones, the singers at the absolute top of their profession— always keep a teacher. Is that true?"

"Why, of course!" he replied.

"Why? Don't you ever learn all that you need?"

He looked at me for a moment and smiled. Then he said, "You don't understand. It is very easy for an opera singer to slip into bad habits without knowing it. And a bad habit can not only damage the purity of your tone; it can even damage your vocal cords. So every skilled singer wants a good teacher who will listen and check what he's doing."

He continued, "Dr. Kinlaw, you know the secret to great singing, don't you?" I assured him I did not. "The secret," he said, " is to let your breath do it all. Singers sometimes try to impose their own unique style instead of letting the breath flow freely. That's how we develop bad habits. The power and purity come when a singer does not get in the way."

As I walked away from that conversation, I realized that I had just heard a masterful sermon on the Christian ministry. This is what God meant when he said that his servants work "not by might, nor by power, but by my Spirit" (Zech 4:6). Then I thought of a familiar passage at the end of Isaiah 40:

> But those who hope in the Lord will renew their strength. They will soar on wings like eagles; they will run and not grow weary, they will walk and not be faint. (Isa 40:31)

The Hebrew verb translated in English as "renew" literally means "to change" or "to exchange" (*halaph*). This same word is used in Genesis 35:2, where God tells Jacob to build an altar and to instruct his people to get rid of their idols, purify themselves, and change (*halaph*) their clothes so they could go up and worship their God. We could just as well translate this familiar verse in Isaiah to say that those who hope in God "will *exchange* their strength" with God's. We may come to God in our own strength, but we want to go away in the strength of the Lord. God's grace does not make us adequate so that we can do the work of God. It cleanses our motives so that God can make us the means and the occasion for what he seeks to do. We are the means and the occasion but never the cause or source of God's eternal work.

We can learn several lessons from this principle. One is that God's grace can never be stored or held in reserve. It is like manna—we need it fresh every day. I learned that about my sermons. Yesterday's sermon, unless I rework it and pray it through again, always has a whiff of rot about it. We cannot serve God with yesterday's anointing. I am sure this was one of the reasons for Paul's "thorn." A man as strong-willed and purposeful as Paul could become proud and self-confident, so God gave him this "thorn" to remind him that everything good about his ministry was God's work and not his own.

Another lesson here is our perpetual need for the Teacher, the Holy Spirit. We need him to check us so that we do not insert ourselves and our wishes into our service or our prayers. We need to hear the Spirit say, "Remember, it's not your will that needs to be done. It's my will and my power that you need." If we heed the voice of our Teacher, we can be sure that it is

- his strength in which we live,
- his prayers that we pray,
- his effectiveness in which we serve,
- his virtue that shines through us, and
- his agape love that marks our ministry.

Too many times I have been more Pelagian than biblical in all of this. Pelagius, a contemporary of Augustine's, believed that we have a free will that enables us to take the initiative to seek God and do God's will in our own strength. However, Jesus made it clear that we are no good on our own (Mark 10:17–18). If any goodness is found in us, it must be God's goodness flowing through us. George MacDonald was thinking of this when he wrote his poem "Smoke":

Lord, I have laid my heart upon thy altar
But cannot get the wood to burn;
It hardly flares ere it begins to falter
And to the dark return.

Old sap, or night-fallen dew, makes damp the fuel;
In vain my breath would flame provoke;
Yet see—at every poor attempt's renewal
To thee ascends the smoke!

'Tis all I have—smoke, failure, foiled endeavour,
Coldness and doubt and palsied lack:
Such as I have I send thee!—perfect Giver,
Send thou thy lightning back.[1]

There is a vast difference between smoke and fire, especially if the fire is lightning.. The smoke is our offering; the fire is God's presence. We don't have to settle for a life of smoke, because God is more eager to give himself than we are to receive him. But the difference between his identity and ours, between his power and our powerlessness, never changes.

I pray that God will remind you of the difference between your strength and his. May you learn what it means to pray in God's strength so that he can pray his prayers through you and so that your strengthlessness will be made perfect in his strength.

---

1. George MacDonald et al., *A Threefold Cord* (London: W. Hughes, 1883).

# 10

## Praying for Revival

GIVE ME ONE DIVINE MOMENT WHEN GOD ACTS,

AND I SAY THAT MOMENT IS FAR SUPERIOR

TO ALL THE HUMAN EFFORTS OF MAN

THROUGHOUT THE CENTURIES.[1]

I invite you to consider the need for a specific type of prayer: the prayer for revival, inviting Christ to come and dwell anew within his people.

Some Christians do not recognize the need for revival because of their theology. They believe that salvation is a one-time gift and they have received it, so what more do they need? Perhaps they can grow in their understanding of the gift and the Giver, but they believe the gift is eternally theirs.

However, if salvation is the personal presence of the Lord Jesus, then revival is needed again and again because all personal relationships need times of refreshing. Particularly after an intensive period of Christian work or ministry, our relationship with the Lord Jesus needs to be refreshed.

*yet our ministry/"work" should be led by the Spirit*

---

1. Dennis F. Kinlaw, as quoted in Robert E. Coleman, *One Divine Moment* (Old Tappan, NJ: Fleming H. Revell, 1970), 5.

In Old Testament times, God commanded that all Jews should gather three times a year in the city of Jerusalem for specific festivals. We find records of this throughout the Bible because Jews continued to do this until Jerusalem was destroyed in AD 70. For example, Acts 2 describes how Jesus' disciples had come together for the second of those great festivals, the Feast of Weeks, when the Holy Spirit was poured out upon them on the day of Pentecost. They had come together because God called them together.

Why did God say his people should travel great distances at great personal sacrifice to come together in this way? Because God can do things for us when we are together that he cannot do when we remain separate and alone. A group of people corporately worshiping God have a spiritual potential that cannot be found in a single person's worship. Groups have a greater potential for transformation, as well as greater accountability for their actions.

I once was riding in an undertaker's car from the funeral home to the cemetery with family members of the elderly man who had died. No other family members attended the funeral other than this nephew and the nephew's wife. I had known the deceased quite well, and he had been remarkable. Being rather wealthy, he had at one time personally supported over one hundred missionaries around the world. As we rode to the cemetery, I began conversing with the nephew, who was the sole heir.

He said, "This is a significant moment for me. I am aware that I will inherit my uncle's wealth, but he has already given me something of infinitely greater value than anything that will come from his estate."

"Really?"

"My wife and I were nominal Episcopalians," he said. "We went to church when it was convenient, but Christianity meant absolutely nothing to us. The only thing that ever bothered us was our uncle, who periodically came to see us. He always wanted to attend church, whether or not we wanted to go. He also had a particular interest in the evangelists who came along, and when an evangelist spoke in our area, he always wanted to go.

"If you're the sole heir of a wealthy man, you find yourself remarkably amenable to his wishes, whether or not they're your wishes," he said with a wry smile. "So when Billy Graham announced a crusade in Syracuse, where we lived, I anticipated a call from my uncle.

"The call came quickly. My uncle said, 'Now, my wife and I want to come up and visit you.' I already knew the date he mentioned would be during Graham's evangelistic crusade. Sure enough, they came and I found myself trapped into going to hear Billy Graham. The four of us sat on the back row in the top seats, as high in the stadium as possible, as far away from the pulpit as we could get.

"I consider myself a fairly rational person," he continued, "so don't ask me to explain what happened next. When they came to the close of that service and started singing a song, I began stumbling down those steps! When I got down to the front, someone nudged me. I turned and saw my wife. That night in that stadium, both of us came to know the living Christ."

Something holy takes place when a group of people come together to seek God. A group of people offer God a possibility that is not always present when we are alone.

## The Importance of Certain Times

Think about how many books of the Bible are books of history. God's people have an interest in theology, philosophy, and ethics, but the largest portion of the Bible is spiritual history. In fact, the foundational book of all Scripture is not a book of theology, at least not in the usual sense, but simply the story of a man whose name we know, who lived in a city whose name we know, who received a call from God. Abraham responded to that call and followed God on a long journey. We know the place to which he traveled. Out of his faithfulness, a family was produced; out of that family came a nation; and out of that nation came the Savior of the world. The first book of the Bible is simply the beginning of that history.

So God is interested in the human use of time. He did not want a year to pass without his people being gathered in his presence at least three times. He wanted his people to know that all of time was his gift for sacred purposes, yet certain times are exceptionally important.

A man once told me about his struggle with alcohol. He was sorry that he had this weakness and often became remorseful and repentant. He would fervently resolve never to touch alcohol again, but he could not master it. Then a moment came when Christ met him in a powerful way in an evangelistic service and changed him so that his alcoholism was gone forever.

God makes certain times infinitely richer than others. Scripture is full of examples of such holy moments. Moses had lived eighty years before he met God in a burning bush, but that moment changed human history. On another day in Moses' life, God led him up a mountain and gave him the tablets of the Law. The course of moral history has not been the same since.

Each year, on a special night called the Passover, Jews celebrate God's deliverance of his people from Egypt. God instructed them to mark all of subsequent time by that moment, so the Passover became the beginning of every year for the Israelites.

God comes decisively at certain moments, and then our lives can never be the same again. I think that is why God gives us times of revival.

In post–World War II America, the traditional revival meeting had an unmatched power when specific churches in specific communities would intentionally set apart two weeks to be with God. The people's first priority was to meet God and to get their hearts clean again. An evangelist would come to the community, the people would gather almost every single night, and in the subsequent days the impact of God's Word grew greater. The potential for spiritual transformation became greater. Out of such meetings could come tremendous spiritual fruit. My own family grew up in a typical Southern community. We had five social classes in our town:

Episcopalians, Presbyterians, Methodists, Baptists, and everyone else. We all knew our place. I went to the Methodist Church four times on Sunday: Sunday school, morning church, Epworth League (for young people), and evening church. (Occasionally, my father would require me to attend Wednesday night prayer meeting too.) So church attendance was the rule in our lives, but there was never any genuine transformation in it.

One day, against his will, my father found himself sitting in a Holiness camp meeting in Georgia. He said to himself, "This is what my family needs." So he took most of our family to that meeting the next year. Everything that I had learned through the years of attending church, which had never come alive to me, suddenly became clear at the end of a camp-meeting Bible study when the teacher asked, "Dennis, are you a Christian?"

She had carefully gotten rid of everybody else, so my peers were gone and I didn't have to put on a front. So I said, "Heavens, no."

If my own mother had asked me that question, I would have lied through my teeth. If my pastor had asked me, I would have lied too. But with her, I was free to be honest. She asked, "Wouldn't you like to be?"

I do not understand the miracle of the new birth. But that morning, when I arose from praying with that little lady, I knew the living Christ. My heart had been transformed. There is eternal potential in certain moments like that.

Such camp meetings are rare nowadays, but God can bring revival in other ways as well. One fall, an Asbury College (now University) student was concerned for the blessing of God on the campus, and soon a group of students began meeting for what they called the Great Experiment. This was a commitment of six students to spend thirty extra minutes with God in prayer and Scripture reading every day for thirty days. They resolved to do whatever God told them to do in his Word and to give a clear witness for him each day. The group met together once a week to hold one another accountable and to pray.

At the beginning of the winter quarter, each of those six students began meeting with six more students for another thirty-day

Great Experiment. At the end of those thirty days, they led the chapel service and all thirty-six of those students sat on the platform. One by one, they described the way God had begun to transform their lives. On each seat in the auditorium was a card of commitment giving other students opportunity to join the Great Experiment and wait on God in this way for thirty days.

The next chapel service was on February 3, 1970. On that day, Jesus Christ came to chapel at Asbury College. The same young lady who organized the Great Experiment asked the college administration for a place where students could meet regularly to pray. They began to have prayer meetings, asking God to come to Asbury. At the end of those prayer meetings, the students would get up from the altar and say to one another, "Do you think he will come today?"

Eventually, they had an all-night prayer meeting. That was enough. They knew Christ was coming. Let me share one student's description of what happened during that revival:

> In these days we have found a power to make bad people good, to make the best people better, and that power is found in Jesus Christ. We have found the answer to the need of the heart of man, corporately and individually. That answer is new life in Christ through repentance for sin, faith in the living Christ, and immediate obedience to his holy will.

## RESULTS OF A REVIVAL

What does God accomplish in a revival? He sets us free, just like he set Israel free. He frees us from immorality, from selfishness, from spiritual bondage of every sort. God also gives us a deeper understanding of his ways and his truth. As I read the book of Acts, I find myself amazed at the difference between the disciples' understanding of Jesus before and after Pentecost. Read the gospel of Mark carefully, and you will find Jesus again and again telling Peter, James, and John, "I am going to a cross. It's necessary for the salvation of the world, so I am telling you before it takes place." But they did not understand what he was talking about until the Spirit came. He brought a deeper understanding of Christ and his work of salvation. Some people assume that revival runs counter to intellectual clarity, but when the Spirit of God touches a person's heart and mind, he allows that person to see things the way they really are. When God comes, we begin to see the truth.

In a time of revival, God calls his people to a new level of obedience. We are supposed to grow in grace, and as we walk with him, he leads us into deeper obedience to him. But God can often place his call upon our hearts more persuasively in a larger group of like-minded believers.

In the course of my life, I have watched many young people go into Christian service. In 1970, 25 percent of the students at Asbury College said they planned to enter some kind of Christian vocation. Then came the outpouring of the Holy Spirit in the revival of 1970. By 1973, 41 percent of Asbury's students were considering some kind of full-time Christian ministry. When Jesus brought revival to that campus, the students began to carry a greater burden for the world.

Indeed, revival leads God's people to give themselves more sacrificially for the world. When we worship God with other people and see them respond to the call of God in their lives, awareness unfolds in our hearts that God might be calling us as well. We ask questions of God that he never had the opportunity to answer before, such as, "What should I be doing in obedience to Christ?" and "What is your call upon my life?" Then God can impress upon our hearts individuals, people groups, and even nations he wants us to begin bearing with him. He can bid us to follow Christ's example and live for something bigger than ourselves.

So I ask you to pray for revival. Will you commit yourself to praying that God will come to the place where you live? Will you obey whatever he asks you to do to make that possible? He listens to the intercessory prayers of his people, and he is eager to come and dwell in our midst.

# 11

## Life Eternal

GOD FASHIONED THE HUMAN BODY

WITH EXQUISITE CARE

BECAUSE HE EVENTUALLY

WOULD HAVE ONE HIMSELF.

On the evening of July 9, 2003, I staggered to my bed as weary in body and soul as I have ever been in my life. My wife of fifty-nine years lay sleeping quietly in our living room in a bed provided by hospice. My son Denny, a doctor, watched over her while she slept. I thought I would sleep for only a few moments before resuming my vigil by her bedside, but my body sank into bed and did not stir until Denny woke me at 3:30 with a whisper. "Dad," he said, "I think this is it."

I walked quietly with him down the hallway into the family room and pulled up my chair as close as I could to her bed. My son periodically checked her pulse. We sat there for about forty-five minutes, and then Denny said, "Dad, she's gone."

Slowly, my beloved wife's body, that object of such sacred love, turned cold, looking and feeling like polished marble. In the pre-dawn stillness, as I watched color drain from Elsie's body, I pondered the sacred meaning of this event. God fashioned the human body with exquisite care because he eventually would have one himself. So I began meditating on the incarnation, and did not anticipate the thoughts that came to mind:

*The eternal Son of God took on a body just like this one. A human body just like Elsie's once contained the second person of the blessed Trinity. God himself in the person of his Son assumed a physical existence like this because he likes us and wants to be with us. He wanted to make it possible for us creatures to live eternally with him. So his incarnation did not stop with his crucifixion and death. When God the Father raised Jesus from the tomb, Christ bore in his resurrected form the scars of the wounds in his hands and side. Today, he still lives in that resurrected body he bears at the right hand of the Father.*

*That means Elsie's body is not a castoff to be forgotten, but a reminder of the resurrection that will enable me to see her again in physical form. That ultimate resurrection will restore creation, all of it, to fulfill what God had in mind even before the creation. The material world will once again be vibrant with life and offer its praise to the God who created it, not to evil and death. We human beings will be God's children in the house of our Father.*

*God made us for an intimacy and communion with him far greater than most of us ever imagined. Death, in whose presence I had been standing, will not be the end of us. Death has been conquered. Its work in Elsie's body will be eternally undone. When God the Creator took on the flesh of the creature in Jesus Christ, the eternal God (who the creeds say is "without body or parts") became one with his creation. The invisible became the visible, and he became so for eternity. If we could peer into the inner life of the triune Godhead today, we would see a human being with a form just like ours, Jesus Christ of Nazareth in his resurrection body. His physical presence there promises us the same kind of intimacy with God. Christ invites us into that relationship.*

Suddenly, the room in which I stood—that quiet little room in Wilmore, Kentucky, where Elsie's death had just occurred—was the anteroom of heaven. I had not lost Elsie. She was more alive than she had ever been, and the love we shared for so long did not end with her physical death. The incarnation of Christ and the triune character of God took on a far deeper meaning for me at Elsie's deathbed than it ever had before.

It had been a year since we became aware that something was wrong in Elsie's body. When the doctors identified the cancer, they did immediate surgery. Those next months were not easy. She had a prolonged episode of shingles, with the intractable pain that often accompanies it. Spells of atrial fibrillation, with heart rates of two hundred, would leave her weak and lifeless. Frankly, I did not believe that she would live to see the new year, but she did. She attended our grandson's wedding, and we celebrated our fifty-ninth wedding anniversary, both on New Year's Eve.

I watched Elsie fight to live and grapple with the questions of death and dying. One day she was ready to go to heaven and wondered why Christ did not take her there. The next day she would be full of hope for recovery and could even talk about our future together. During those months, I came to the conclusion that human beings are made for life. Something within us insists, rationally or not, that death is an alien force that does not really belong in our bodies. The God who made us is the God of the living, and all life comes from him. Indeed, physical death entered his world contrary to his will. I thought, *God made us for life because he made us for himself, and he is life. He wants us to be a part of his eternal existence.* And I worshiped in spite of my circumstances.

## The Familial Life of God

Elsie's struggle with death caused me to reflect again on why God has given us physical bodies and why he chose to have one himself. God's life is not solitary. Our language describes it as the union of the three persons of the Trinity: the Father, the Son-of-the-Father, and the Spirit-of-the-Father-and-of-the-Son. Individuality or aloneness has not characterized the God we worship. No person in the Godhead has ever experienced total solitude—except the Son, when he tasted the consequences of our sin in desolation on the cross. Otherwise, God's life has always been triune.

Really, the language of Scripture and our creeds call it a *familial* life. We learned this when God's Son chose to become Mary's son, Jesus. For about thirty years he lived among us as one of us and then began several years of intimate fellowship with his disciples. The apostle John, who was one of those disciples, tells us how close they were:

> That which was from the beginning, which we have *heard,* which we have *seen with our eyes,* which we have *looked at* and *our hands have touched*—this we proclaim concerning the Word of life. The life appeared; we have seen it and testify to it, and we proclaim to you the eternal life, which was with the Father and has appeared to us. (1 John 1:1–2, emphasis added)

It was a fellowship so intimate and joyous that the disciples hoped it would never end. Jesus himself assured them that no one could ever take them from him (John 10:29). Among the last words Jesus uttered before his arrest was a prayer to his Father that his disciples would be where he was (John 17:24). As the Twelve learned more about who he actually was, they grew more confident that he wanted to be with them as much as they wanted to be with him. They saw in Jesus an invitation from the triune God—to them and to all who would come to know God through them—to enter the eternal fellowship the divine family enjoys with one another.

## An Eternal Relationship

I love the way the Old Testament speaks about this eternal relationship. Unfortunately, God must use our "creaturely language," the language of finite space and time, when he talks to us about eternal things. We do not have any vocabulary for eternity because the concept exceeds the limits of our human experience, yet Holy Scripture points us toward that reality. The English word *eternity* simply means "everlasting" or "without end," but the eternity God knows is far more than endlessness. The Old Testament word commonly used to denote eternity is often translated as "an eon" or "an age," but it literally means "for an age and unto _____" (e.g., Isa 46:3–4). The fact that the biblical writers did not put an object after the preposition for "unto" simply indicates that the future with God is completely open.[1] No end is in sight when we come into Christ and Christ comes into us. The life we gain in Christ is eternal life because it is God's life. John calls it an eternal fellowship because, he insists, "our fellowship is with the Father and with his Son, Jesus Christ" (1 John 1:3). That life comes to us through the eternal Son; through him we get into that eternal family. Since God has such love for us, it is little wonder that John feels we should love God.

But then John affirms something even more dramatic. Not only had the disciples found entry into the divine family, but others can enter that fellowship through these new members of the family—through John himself and the others who had already come to know God. As God's witnesses, they are charged to invite everyone into the priceless fellowship they enjoy. Note John's specific words. He says that God's invitation is not first of all to fellowship with God, but to the fellowship of believers of which he is a part. In this fellowship, John says, others can find God:

> We proclaim to you what we have seen and heard, so that you also may have fellowship with us. And our fellowship is with the Father and with his Son, Jesus Christ. We write this to make our joy complete. (1 John 1:3–4)

The implication is clear. Jesus brought his disciples into personal fellowship with God. Then they became the means through which others were introduced to Christ and entered into the "life-together-with-God" they found. Perhaps we should not be surprised at this. Our normal means of getting to know a person is through another. John says it works this way with the family of God too. The normal

---

1. We hear an echo of this Old Testament idiom in Matthew 28:20 (NKJV), where Jesus tells his disciples, "Lo, I am with you always, *even* to the end of the age."

way anyone comes to know God is through someone already in God's family.

The typical Christian will immediately respond, "I understand. You are saying that every Christian should be a witness." Certainly, but also much more.

Children do not enter this world through the mere verbal witness of their parents. They cannot be born into this world by virtue of their parents' describing it to them. They enter the world because someone bears them in her own body for a time, at personal inconvenience and risk, until they can break into this new environment. John says in his gospel that the way to enter the divine family is through spiritual birth, a process that is in many ways remarkably like physical birth (see John 3:3–7). The eternal Son bore us in his heart until we could be delivered into eternity through his atoning sacrifice on the cross. Now the Holy Spirit seeks those who will bear others into the divine family.

Remember, God's Son did not come down *de novo* on a cloud from heaven. He came through a humble Jewish girl named Mary. Through her, God gave his Son to the world. People come from nonexistence into spiritual life through a very similar process in someone else. It begins with a spiritual *conception*—a work of the Holy Spirit in which God's burden for someone else is placed in our hearts. It continues with a *bearing*—we bear the needs of that person, much as a mother bears a child, through intercessory prayer. It culminates in a *delivery*—conversion, that moment when "the new birth" is complete. The whole process depends on our living in such intimacy with God that he, through his Spirit, can put the burdens of other people into our hearts. Then we become the means through which a world can come to know Christ.

I trust this book has helped you to see that the spiritual world works in this way. Consider how you can join God in his redemptive work. Remember that it begins, continues, and comes to consummation in a life of prayer.

# SCRIPTURE INDEX